ArtEZ Press / *d'*jongeHond

Dear relation,

It is with great pleasure that we present you this publication *Beyond Green*. We hope this book will stimulate the way of thinking about sustainability and create new ideas. Hopefully it inspires the further development of sustainability in clothing.

Control Union, an independent certifier of sustainable products and processes, played a modest role in making this book. Furthermore, we facilitated the availability of the book for students on the dutch Academies, there the creativity in sustainability begins!

Control Union World Group,

**Johan Maris
Mark Prosé
Gijs van der Lee**

746.9 BEY

contents

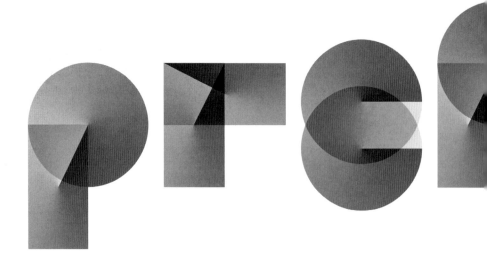

SUSTAINABLE BREAKS THROUGH!

'Everybody who was in eco fashion looked like a bag of potatoes', declared David Shah, the well-known fashion designer, trend watcher and moderator at the *Beyond Green* fashion symposium about ethical fashion at the end of 2007. That all belongs to the past - eco fashion is the cutting-edge trend and the future.

That's the thing: sustainability as a trend and as a lifestyle, in everything we do and thus in everything we wear. This is why it was my pleasure to open a 'sustainable' fashion show in the foyer of my ministry in June this year. The ethical, sustainable and beautiful clothing on the catwalk impressed me. I saw it as a sign that the fashion world is embracing sustainability. And even more importantly, ethical and sustainable are hot items among trendsetting consumers. This is evident from the rising sales figures, the enormous amount of new eco labels and the great demand for organic cotton and new sustainable synthetic fibres.

Fashion companies have in recent years become much more aware of bad labour and environmental conditions in the clothing industry. Badly paid and unhealthy child labour in sweat shops, the use of insecticides, pesticides and polluting dyes - it is not just action groups and environmental organisations that are denouncing these. The clothing branch is itself taking action. Companies are realising that publicity about abuses can seriously damage their labels. And they are also discovering that sustainability and fairness makes their companies stronger and more social. Good labour conditions, a better environment and clarity concerning the chains from raw material to product in the shop are much more often at the top of the agenda in the boardrooms of famous clothing companies.

Are sustainability and fairness a hype? I don't think so. Fashion is experience.

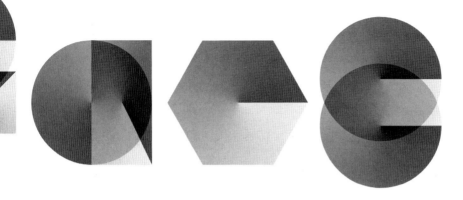

It is supposed to make you 'feel good'. 'Feeling good' is about more than just appearance. Who would want to buy those beautiful trousers if they're associated with scandals about exploitation and poisoning? In the meantime, many sustainable fashion companies have understood this and are showing that sustainable fashion really does work and can be commercially successful. And fortunately there are a lot of these leading companies nowadays: from Brennels to M'Braze, from Cora Kemperman to YOI guerilla store. Or take the company Dutch Spirit Fashion which is making new jeans from old ones according to the 'Cradle to Cradle' principle.

Sustainability has to be passed on from the trendsetters to the entire fashion and clothing industry. Fashion education has an important role in this. Today's students, after all, are the designers and purchasers of tomorrow. They hold the key to anchoring sustainability in the fashion world through the application of new technology and ecologically-aware designs and purchasing policies. That can only work if they learn to deal with eco-technology and new, sustainable materials, if they learn to recognise the social and ecological aspects of fashion.

Finally, this book is largely based on the lectures that were given during the *Beyond Green* symposium. One conclusion from both the symposium and this book is clear: people, planet and profit are getting more in balance in the fashion world. This is a trend that should be entrenched and extended. All parties - the fashion companies, fashion education, social organisations, action groups, knowledge institutions and governments - must continue working towards ethical, sustainable fashion. Hip and honest - it requires hard work. This book offers a great deal of inspiration for this. I hope you enjoy reading it!

Dr. Jacqueline M. Cramer
Dutch Minister of Spatial Planning and the Environment

Sustainability and corporate social responsibility (CSR) are becoming increasingly important in the fashion world. Fashion designers and fashion companies are more and more often confronted with critical social organisations and consumers who want to know where and how their clothing is made. Governments, too, are demanding that companies conform to higher standards. Designers, product developers and buyers are devoting more and more importance to social and ecological aspects when selecting their materials, colours and production methods. Many initiatives in this area have been launched.

In order to make an essential contribution to the discussion around this theme, AMFI Amsterdam Fashion Institute, ArtEZ Institute of the Arts (dAcapo-ArtEZ department of general studies and ArtEZ Professorship of Fashion) and Modebewust organised the symposium *Beyond Green, Progress in Fashion and Sustainability*, which was held on November 14 2007 in the World Fashion Center (WFC) in Amsterdam. The *Beyond Green* book consists largely of edited versions of the lectures and presentations given by various national and international specialists. This material is supplemented with interviews and existing

articles that represent various points of view on the state of affairs with regard to fashion and sustainability. Besides thematic approaches to 'fashion and sustainability', there are also examples from fashion practice, articles about clean production methods and practical information and addresses.

The editors of this book hope that the essays, interviews and contributions by fashion designers included here will inspire the development of a vision that goes further than 'green' as just another fashion trend.

We wish to express our thanks to Control Union, which certifies sustainable products and processes and whose financial contribution helped to facilitate the production of this book and its availability for students in further education.

Jan Brand
Tine Luyt
Minke Vos

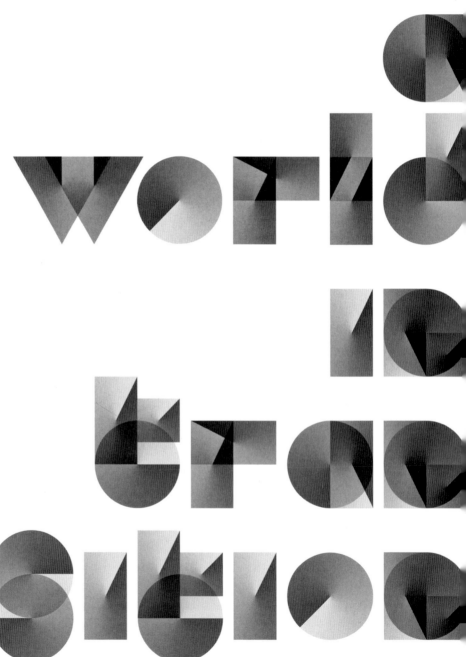

world in transition

ONE ARMCHAIR BY JORIS LAARMAN (WWW.JORISLAARMAN.COM). MORE DESIGNERS
RE LOOKING TO NATURE, NOT RETROGRESSIVELY, BUT RATHER TO UNDERSTAND THE
OMPLEXITY, EFFICIENCY AND DURABILITY OF NATURAL SUBSTANCES. RESEARCHERS AT
UEENS UNIVERSITY BELFAST AND UNIVERSITY OF LEEDS ARE WORKING TO DEVELOP
OLOGICAL CEMENTS THAT MIMIC THE PROPERTIES OF BONE AND CAN BE USED TO
PAIR SPINAL INJURIES. FURNITURE AND PRODUCT DESIGNERS ARE SIMILARLY COMBINING
NTHETIC MATERIALS WITH BIOMETRIC PROCESSES. THE RESULTS INCLUDE JORIS LAARMAN'S
ONE FURNITURE RANGE. 'TREES HAVE THE ABILITY TO ADD MATERIAL WHERE STRENGTH IS
EEDED', EXPLAINS LAARMAN. 'BUT BONES ALSO HAVE THE ABILITY TO TAKE AWAY MATERIAL
HERE IT IS NOT NEEDED.'

We are living in a world of transition. We are bogged down with recession and we are confused, but at the same time we are looking for a new start. Sometimes, however, we are looking for solutions in the wrong places. Our gut reaction to crises can be emotional rather than rational, sentimental rather than realistic. Take the whole 'eco' issue. Still, too many people lump climate change, ecology, sustainability, fair trading and ethics in the same bag – when, actually they are different issues, each with its own very significant role to play towards a common goal. People have become nostalgic, even Luddite in their thinking. We are bogged down with the concept of 'organic' and the concept that only things grown in a totally natural way can be good. Is that so? Isn't it time to drop our 'Frankenfoods' approach to genetically modified crops? As Tony Blair, Britain's ex-Prime Minister said, 'We must put our hopes for the future in the hands of scientists.'

Just look what happened to the bio-fuel phenomenon. Palm oil and ethanol were not only better for the environment, but a way to combat unstable oil prices. Now, it seems that the emerging multi-billion dollar bio-fuel industry could bring with it huge sacrifices in bio-diversity, food shortages and an increase in poverty unless it is carefully managed.

THE SYNTHETIC FUTURE[1]

If you think we have come a long way in the last fifty years, forget it! Very soon, we will transfer information by thought, run faster and further without tiring and orgasm on demand. For the first time in history the fields of neuroscience, bio-mechanics, robotics, mathematics, computer science, materials science, tissue engineering and nanotechnology are starting to merge and share their expertise on an unprecedented scale. The result is a whole new world. Just take nanotechnology. Within a decade, molecular manufacturing will produce goods one atom at a time making cars and medical implants as strong as steel and light as a feather. Eventually industry will be able to replicate any material including food, water and energy; in medicine nanorobots will manipulate atoms to neutralize cancer, viruses and bacteria.

Prospects in the field of bio-enhancement are even more amazing. Brain chip technology is already well developed, but how much further can we take it? Could we eventually link a cochlear implant to the internet, thus extending the nervous system as far as the web takes it? Receive phone calls by ear? Have infinite memory? As Francis Fukuyama already noted in 2002, we are entering a period of post-human change - a place in which people and their chimera roam side by side - one providing organs, skin and regenerative transplants for the other in an owner/slave relationship. And, meanwhile, we will be having intercourse with robots by 2050, if we are to believe chess champion and author, David Levy.

None of this is hypothetical. One million Americans now use reclaimed tissues to rejuvenate their bodies. In Japan, the growth of the so-called partner robot industry is becoming a multi-million yen industry. Of course, much of this raises some very serious ethical, moral and social issues – not least on how the rich and powerful could benefit at the cost of the poor and how far Man should go in playing God!

It is clear that to make technology work for us rather than overpower us, we are going to have to rebuild some of those very boundaries technology has taken down. It is also clear that we need to be prepared for the risks that may go hand in hand with technological advances. Before we rush into future solutions – no matter how beneficial they seem to mankind – we should be examining the potential consequences and carefully assessing their impact.

On the other hand, technological advances are like Pandora's Box. In the classical Greek myth, Pandora, through sheer curiosity and desire, opened a box releasing all the evils of mankind – greed, vanity, slander, envy, pining – leaving only hope inside, as she struggled to close everything up again. What is done cannot be undone, what is known cannot be unknown.

LESS IS MORE

Of course, science is not going to solve everything. If we are going to create a better Earth, we are going to have to take a hard look at our current lifestyles and make Draconian choices – eat less, travel less, consume less and, yes, have less babies! Have you ever asked yourself how many items of clothing you have in your wardrobe and never worn? Or why you need to own more than thirty pairs of shoes? Some facts make staggering reading. For example, between 2001 and 2005, the number of garments bought per person in the UK increased by over one-third. Estimates differ as to how much is discarded. DEFRA says 1.1 million tonnes of textiles are thrown away in household bins every year, whereas a recent report by the Institute for Manufacturing at Cambridge University puts the figure higher, at 1.8 million tonnes of textiles. To put it in perspective, a single tonne of textiles fills roughly two hundred black bin bags. Imagine 220 million black bin bags sent to landfill and you get an idea of why we should reduce our buying, reuse and recycle. According to Wastewatch, two million shoes are thrown in rubbish bins in the UK every week. For too long now, society has been arguing that more means better – more possessions, more work, more information, more success. Now, more and more people understand the need to apply the breaks and to start a life of self-limitation – not just because of planet sustainability, but also because trying to 'have it all' only causes burnout, stress, depression. 'shopping coma', 'consumer adultery', and 'affluenza' are all new stress diseases apparently caused by affluence.

You can already see this approach in new attitudes to luxury in the OECD

'GENETIC TRACE' BY SUSANA SOARES PREDICTS A FUTURE WHERE PEOPLE WILL BE EQUIPPE
WITH SPECIALLY DESIGNED ORGANS THAT ACT AS PERCEPTION ENHANCERS, ALLOWIN
THEM TO COLLECT GENETIC MATERIAL DURING INTERPERSONAL ENCOUNTERS. 'HAIRY' NAIL
WILL SCRAPE DEAD CELLS FROM OTHERS WHEN SHAKING HANDS. WWW.SUSANA.SOARES.CO

CHEFS AND SCIENTISTS ARE EXPERIMENTING WITH TWO-DIMENSIONAL FOODS TO ALLC
CUSTOMERS TO TRY OUT NEW FLAVOURS. THIS IDEA WILL BE DEVELOPED TO ENABLE PEOP
TO PRINT THEIR OWN FLAVOURS. CHICAGO CHEF HOMARO CANTU HAS CREATED AN INK-J
PRINTER WHICH PRODUCES EDIBLE IMAGES. ILLUSTRATION BY MOTOTAKE MAKISHIM

countries where bling and ostentation have been completely forsaken for con-spicuous abstention, discretion, privacy, philanthro-capitalism, discernment, connoisseurship, knowledge and emotional content. You can also see it in the changing behavioural patterns of lifestyle groups. Boomers (1946-1964) invented consumerism and, although many will continue to work, aspire and collect until their dying days, many are 'cashing in their career earnings' for something they want to do, embracing self-sufficiency, material simplicity and personal development. Meanwhile, Gen X, Grups or the Bridge Generation (accounting for 48 million Americans alone born between 1965 and 1976) are busy striving to find a new balance between work/money and personal life by telecommuting, working fewer hours and even quitting their jobs to spend more time with their family.

A DIVIDED WORLD

Of course, not all people are thinking in the same way at the same time. In Chi-na, India, Brazil and Russia and other fast growing economies, the large num-bers of wealthy and the booming middle class are all at stage one on the luxury ladder, where acquisition means status and excessive equals success. And it's not only the developing world that is still hungry to consume. The value of the 'budget' clothing market in the UK (i.e., Primark, Tesco, Matalan, Asda, TK Maxx) has increased by 45 percent over the past five years to more than £6 billion and the sector is growing at twice the rate of the normal clothing market. Still, there is a ground swell and a growing desire by 'prosumers' and 'wealthier' customers to create a viable economic alternative to exponential, economic growth. That means, we are looking at a fast dividing consumer society – not just geographi-cally, East and West, but also along class divisions. As Sweden's David Report (http//davidreport.com issue #9) contends: 'we see the contours of a new class system, where the privileged and well-off buy environmentally friendly, durable and regionally produced goods, while your "average Joe" is busy with lavish and irresponsible spending on goods *Made in China*.'

The UK's market research group, Mintel, seems to back up that way of think-ing. According to the company, 'value clothing' is now at the heart of British shopping in spite of concerns over sustainability and ethical sourcing. Two in five adults now admit to buying their 'basics' at 'value' shops rather than the occasional piece like party dresses. Analysts are forecasting market growth of nearly forty percent to reach a record £8.7 billion by 2012.

So, if we are to really build an alternative system of consuming, how to go about it? Firstly, there can be no discussion about giving up on consuming. We, the economy and, eventually the Earth cannot survive without consump-tion. It's just that we will consume in a different and more responsible way. The responsibility factor starts with demanding a new relationship with companies.

THE 'ORICALCO' SHAPE MEMORY SHIRT BY GRADO ZERO ESPACE CAN BE PROGRAMMED SO THE SLEEVES SHORTEN IMMEDIATELY AS THE ROOM TEMPERATURE INCREASES.

No one is blinded by brand aura and marketing messages anymore. What is demanded are transparency, authenticity and dialogue with 'aware' manufacturers.

ETHICS & SUSTAINABILITY

This comes through in the growing demand for fair and ethical trading practices. As said in a recent *Elle* UK article, 'Can Fashion have a Conscience?': 'It's gone beyond questioning what is in our food. People want transparency about the manufacturing of other products. They want to know that their clothes tell a good story.'

The BBCis planning an on-line ethical fashion magazine called *Thread* in tandem with a four-part TV programme called *Blood, Sweat and T-shirts*. According to a recent report from the Co-op Bank, spending on 'ethical' goods and services has almost doubled in the UK in the last five years. The total UK ethical market is now worth £32.3 billion, nine percent more than a year ago, even though it's still only a fraction of total consumer spending of more than £600 billion. Sustainability and 'cradle to cradle' thinking is another big factor. With landfill such a big issue, more and more companies should be winning over customers by promoting recycling initiatives, i.e., offering clients small payments for returning old clothes for reprocessing or turning old jeans into, say, denim sandals, old leather jackets into new leather bags.

Core to this whole new pattern of consumption is buying less but buying better – in terms of quality, lifespan and sustainability, sustainability in terms of avoiding landfill by knowing that someone else will want the things you no longer care for. Thus, we will look harder for true favourites, for products that we do not tire of – the super normal, the extra ordinary, where content triumphs over style and products represent socially responsible design, based on quality, reliability and responsibility. After all, no one has ever bettered the paper clip or the angle-poise lamp (both, incidentally, invented in the 1930s, another period of depression and hardship).

We will come to understand the difference between 'value' and 'values' in clothing. Tired by the stratospheric prices of designer brands or the monotony of High Street cloning and discount pricing we are seeking a new middle-market, sensible level of clothes. The feeling that 'less is more' and longevity and sustainability are all important will be reflected in the way we buy more vintage clothing, share wardrobes and swap garments. As Jeremy Rifkin argued ten years ago, we will finally move into 'the age of access', away from an economy in which it was good to own stuff into one in which people prefer to rent it. Sharing costs, partial ownership, renting will get bigger and bigger. In the end, retailers might end up earning more from servicing rather than producing and selling.

This is a whole new world of consuming we are discussing. The question is how many companies are ready for such a challenging shift in behaviour –

especially in today's economic climate. Equally important, how many people are prepared to accept a 'Brave New World' where science and the synthetic is seen and appreciated in the same light as nature and the organic. Again, as the David Report #9 puts it, 'Up until now, it has not been an exaggeration to say, "The one who has the most things when he dies wins." But, the power of consumption is being questioned and there's a change in attitude and way of life. A suitable expression for the future could be, "The one with the most insight when he dies wins."'

[1]   For more information see *Viewpoint* #22, 'Our Synthetic Future', www.view-publications.com.

E WILL BE HAVING INTERCOURSE WITH ROBOTS BY 2050, IF WE ARE TO BELIEVE CHESS
HAMPION AND AUTHOR, DAVID LEVY.

GGAN MORRIS ARCHITECTS WINNING DESIGN FOR LIVERPOOL OBSERVATORY AIMS TO
CARBON NEUTRAL. PHOTO-LUMINESCENT MATERIAL WOULD BE INCORPORATED INTO
BUILDING, ALLOWING THE STRUCTURE TO GLOW WITHOUT THE NEED FOR ARTIFICIAL
HTING. WWW.DUGGANMORRISARCHITECTS.COM

JOSÉ TEUNISSEN

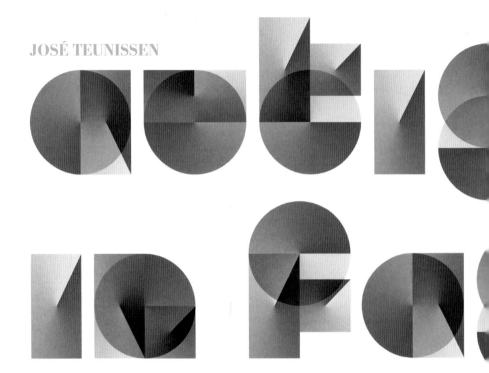

ORSON & BODIL,
SKIRTS, 1992

INTRODUCTION

Eco is back in fashion! The trend reached its peak for the first time in the early 1990s. The ambitions at that time were very high. People wanted to change fashion on a permanent basis by making it durable and timeless. But one of the essential qualities of the fashion system is that it is constantly changing, renewing itself each time anew. That is how I described it sixteen years ago. At that time I didn't see any essential change happening in the system. And indeed, in the course of time, attention waned and H&M's and Esprit's eco-collections vanished from the assortment as quickly as they had arrived.

Yet the ecological awareness has indeed continued to make itself felt under the surface all these years. More than I had suspected at the time. Now that concern for ecological clothing is blossoming again and is widely being picked up by the fashion labels, it is becoming clear that a great deal of progress has been made in all these years in the fields of technology, working conditions and awareness of effects on the environment.

In 1992 people still pictured the future in terms of naturally dyed, ecological cotton. Today there are numerous natural fibres that require much less intensive agriculture and irrigation - think of bamboo, hemp and stinging-nettle. Thanks to technological innovations in the laboratory we can now also make an unprecedently popular new 'fleece' fabric from recycled pet bottles that are indeed actually less harmful for the environment than natural fibres. The nineties saw the first use of closed baths for dyeing and finishing garments like jeans with polluting substances. Before that, the waste water was simply discharged into open rivers. That too has become unthinkable nowadays.

During the last sixteen years the whole circulation system of fashion has been structurally reviewed. In 1992 Esprit was still promoting handmade glass buttons from Ghana, as I describe below, without worrying about the 'journey miles'. The buttons went from Ghana to the Netherlands and then on to India to be sewn onto clothing and then back to Europe. Just as with biological food, the fashion industry now has quality marks and controls, so that origin, trajectory and labour conditions can easily be traced. The public's general opinion has changed so much that even major companies like C&A explain on their website that their products are 'ethically' sound. h&m, too, is about to launch a collection made from ecological cotton produced by a local cooperative in Uganda. Although the visible aspect of the ecology trends disappeared in the mid-nineties, its 'ethical' aspect has actually become more intense.

In recent years, however, new labels have appeared on the market that express their eco awareness in their brand profile. In the Netherlands we have the jeans label Kuyichi, and noir is developing at rapid speed in Denmark, but an existing labels like Filippa k is also bringing out a lingerie line made of ecological cotton and Levi's has eco jeans in its range.

The most remarkable thing about the current eco trend is that it looks completely different from the trend of the nineties. At that time the ecological collections were mainly made of unbleached and undyed cotton and people tried to give them as timeless a look as possible by going for classic shirts, tunics or a trench coat. Eco fashion thus had a clean, minimalist and timeless look. Today's ecological fashion has a radically different aesthetic. The challenge now for designers is to make fabrics and clothes look just as sexy and glamorous as 'conventional' fashion. You are not supposed to tell any more from how it looks whether the fabric and its manufacture are ecological and the working conditions correct. The association with goat's wool socks and the classic Fair Trade shop has to be avoided. For ecology is presenting itself as hip and sexy. The pop star Bono, for example, has his fair trade label Edun and designer Stella McCartney is sympathetic towards ecology. This eco trend is hence a good deal more cheerful and elegant than the previous one. What was formerly a lifestyle connected with leftwing ideals has now become a self-evident way of life and a marketing principle – without doom-mongering and without radical action groups.

In what follows I describe how a new attitude towards clothing arose among designers in the early nineties, and how other aspects of an item of clothing became important. A number of avant-garde designers in those years no longer concentrated on a spectacular appearance, but on comfort and/or subtle details. Martin Margiela, for example, built up a reputation by making ingenious new garments from second-hand clothes. In his view, the wear and tear of second-hand brought more poetry and dimensions to the resulting design, apart from the positive effect on the environment. Alexander van Slobbe likewise devoted a lot of attention to the garment itself in these years with his Orson & Bodil label. The technique of making, the craftsmanship and small, subtle details were central. They gave the designs a lasting quality and several details were so subtle that only the wearer was aware of them. The revival of haute couture by all the classic French fashion houses that started in 1996 is a logical consequence of this renewed appreciation of the garment itself and its quality.

Fashion will not really become durable because of this. But, over the course of the years, what have become much more important are the quality, the craftsmanship and the intrinsic values of the product. As a result, an outfit no longer has to be thrown away after just one season, but lasts for years because of its timeless quality. What was avant-garde has now, almost twenty years later, become generally accepted by many labels. This means that the eco trend of the nineties has finally delivered something after all.

Design using leather, silk and
certified fair trade cotton,
from the Noir Autumn/
Winter 2007 Collection.
Noir aims to "turn corporate
social responsibility sexy" by
combining luxury fashion with
meaningful enterprise for
trade not aid.

22

KUYICHI,
SPRING/SUMMER 2008

APOC ISSEY MIYAKE,
EXHIBITION *MAKING THINGS*,
TOKYO, 2000

POSTER FOR
ETHICAL FASHION SHOW,
PARIS, 2007

'EVERYTHING HAS TO CHANGE IN ORDER TO STAY THE SAME.'

(Alain Delon as Tancredi to Burt Lancaster as the Prince in
Il Gattopardo, 1963, Luchino Visconti)

The current malaise in the fashion industry cannot be completely ascribed to a stagnating economy, since the reason for the decline in turnover is only partly due to the recession. Consumers in the nineties are voluntarily spending less, suggesting that their attitude towards fashion has radically changed. The fashionable, materialistic yuppie only interested in showing off no longer exists. Many people have become convinced that there is an ecological crisis and it has become 'fashionable' to live soberly and to focus attention onto so-called sensible products made from environmentally-friendly materials.

The Research Institute on Social Change (RISC) recently found that the nineties consumer has matured and is tired of constantly changing her appearance.[1] She no longer allows herself to be seduced by a beautiful image or an attractive look. The quality of the product itself has become more important than its design. Products that have proved their value in the past are particularly popular. This can clearly be seen from the revival of brogues, the Burberry, jeans and white shirts. People prefer to wear well-made evergreens that are 'authentic' and 'timeless' rather than an extravagant product that goes out of fashion after just one season. Today's consumer is looking for 'sensible' products. 'Quality' and 'ecologically responsible' have become key concepts. Also when it comes to buying clothes the consumer has to have the idea that it is a matter of a lasting investment. Instead of a complete new wardrobe the modern consumer only purchases separate items that match what she already has at home in the cupboard. The eighties, in which status, money and image were chic, have been superseded by an era dominated by morality and a sober lifestyle. Luxury goods can indeed ensure status, but in a decade in which it is a question of the personality of the user, they express little. What matters now is what you have to say and your attitude to life. Taste and distinction are expressed in spirituality, being well-read and a conscious way of life and this has little to do with a dazzling appearance.

You would expect that the fashion industry would regard this changed mentality as a downright catastrophe. It is after all in its interest to sell as many clothes as possible. And the more frequently and faster the fashion trends succeed one another, the more sales there are. But, strangely enough, major fashion com-

24

panies including Esprit, Benetton and Hennes & Mauritz are precisely taking advantage of this new fashion mentality. Esprit and Benetton even exhort their customers in their advertisements to consume less. Does this mean that the fashion industry has repented and is putting social responsibility above profits? Or does it mean that they are zeroing in on the spirit of the times in a very sophisticated way, only to switch over to the next trend as soon as the environment boom is over? Judging from the prognoses,[2] the industry is indeed assuming its responsibility and a number of fundamental changes will occur in the fashion system. The influential trends magazine *View* noted this change already in 1989, but in 1992 had to acknowledge that it had not expected the change to be so radical. Like other industries, the textile industry is starting to realise on a major scale that all good things must come to an end. It is finally getting through to people that there is a dark side to capitalism and the technological achievements of western society. Through unbridled materialism and ever-increasing consumption we are not only exhausting our planet's resources but also thoroughly disturbing the ecological balance. Both the public and industry are now starting to realise that the blinkered mentality of the last decades – live for today, care for today – can no longer be maintained. The logical consequence of this is that people have started to comment on the fashion system. Fashion is, after all, the consumption article par excellence. A lot of the clothes that we purchase are in order to look different, not because we need them. Trend forecasters are claiming that fashion and clothing will radically change under the influence of ecological awareness and will even acquire a very different interpretation in the future.[3] We are approaching a time when clothing will have little to do with a constantly changing external appearance, but much more with sustainability and timelessness. Instead of an emphatic aesthetic intended to show off or to convey status, clothes in the future will have to suggest a sober and honest look, to emanate an ethical awareness. Clothing is becoming the expression of a conscious and environmentally-friendly way of life and of a sincere personality who listens to her desires and regards it as unimportant whether she impresses others with her appearance.

We might ask ourselves whether this change in fashion mentality, which is presented under the general heading of 'eco-trend', is really as responsible, 'pure' and 'authentic' as the fashion magazines, shops and interiors would have us believe. Can products be really timeless or natural or is that just the image that is given out? And do we really want to live consciously and responsibly as consumers or does a purchased product only have to suggest 'responsibility'? In other words, is ecology the umpteenth new trend or are we dealing with a genuine revolution?

In order to be able to answer these questions it is important to first take a look at what fashion actually means in our culture today. Roland Barthes says in *Système de la mode* that, under its layer of superficiality, the external phenomenon of fashion harbours essential aspects of culture.[4] Since time immemorial the body has been modeled after an ideal form. Every period has its own ideal of beauty, which we can retrace in photographs, paintings and sculptures depicting both clothed and unclothed bodies. As Philippe Perrot also states, the ideas and desires under discussion at a particular period automatically leave their mark on amorphous flesh.[5] What he means by this is that, lying hidden behind the clothing prescriptions and constantly changing forms of fashion, are ideas about behaviour and hygiene, about a society's deep-seated ideas and desires. But fashion and clothing not only reflect the spirit of the times; they are, according to Barthes, a language in which the individual says something about his or her identity. Anyone who has ever been on a nudist beach will know how difficult it is to say what these sun worshippers do in everyday life. But as soon as they are clothed all sorts of associations come to mind about their profession, personality and status. Professional clothing works particularly efficiently in that respect. We immediately know when we answer the door if we're dealing with the postman or with the plumber. But judgments about someone's personality or political and social ideas also present themselves automatically. We would not expect a man in an austere suit to be a welfare worker or someone with socialist ideals. These meanings change or become nuanced over the course of the years under the influence of changing fashions or group cultures. Right now, the clothes worn by Felix Rottenberg perfectly express the new PvdA mentality. His dark blue Hugo Boss suit gives him 'new left' managerial references, but combined with an open-necked shirt and braces there still lies a remnant of familiar leftwing socialist slovenliness. The meanings and codes of clothing are constantly changing, but the basic idea behind clothing and appearance remains: appearance is regarded as a mirror of the inner self, as a sign of character, personality, status and political ideals.[6] At the same time Barthes sees a further function for clothing behaviour, one that in fact contradicts the previous one but which is necessary in order to be able to escape the all too strict demands imposed by the yoke of culture. This is the considerable personal pleasure that fashion allows one to indulge in. Fashion gives the ego the freedom to continually play with identities. A definitive choice never has to be made - a person's identity can be altered per season, per day, per moment. Fashion actually makes this easy. Simply by changing the right detail you transform yourself into another type. Jeans and shirt combined with boots instantly evokes a tough cowboy look, while the same ensemble in combination with a leather jacket suggests the idea of a fifties biker. Through constantly changing our appearance we can escape our personality and take on other qualities. Clothes thus help us to expand the boundaries of the ego. 'They testify to a dream of wholeness, according to which the human being can be everything at once and not has to choose', says Roland Barthes.[7] It is the same pleasure in escapism that we experience with a film or a novel, in which we can surrender to the dream of being a different person. Elizabeth Wilson explains this form of escapism in more psychological terms, as an expression of a fundamental desire to regard one's own body as immutable and immortal. Fashion's permanent fixation on a new and different appearance sophisticatedly diverts attention from the concrete body that gradually becomes older, shriveled and more and more sagging.[8]

As is evident from the aforementioned views, fashion is essentially changeable. Not only are the constantly changing norms, ideas and desires of an era reflected in our external appearance, but fashion also fulfils a number of modern man's essential desires to constantly transform one's own personality, one's own body and identity. The current ecological trend standing for lasting and timeless clothing may have radical consequences in this respect. The principle of changes in clothing is being curbed and in the most extreme case this will lead to the disappearance of fashion. The ecological trend means that we can swathe ourselves indefinitely in a white shirt, a soutane or a wrapover. These are all garments whose form is so sober that they transcend any desire for a fashionable or designer look. They promise never to become outdated or to be boring. Lidewij Edelkoort sees this taking shape, for example, in uniform tunics that can be worn by men, women and children. But is such a thing possible? Should fashion cease changing in the future then it will have radical consequences for culture. How then will we be able to express the spirit of the times? Or has the spirit of the times become redundant in the post-ecological era of sustainability? And more importantly, how will people be able to satisfy their need for masquerade and different identities? After all, the ecology trend promises only more of the same! This is why, besides the ecology trends, we are also seeing strong counter-trends emerging in fashion. Camp, kitsch and excess, kinky rubber and 'to travesty history' in the deconstruction style of Cindy Sherman are also playing a role in fashion. Strangely enough – and at the same time typical of fashion – these trends exist independently of each other. They are open to all and not exclusively reserved for people sharing the same ideology. You can wear a sober, ecologically responsible outfit during the day and then go out in the evening in a bizarre, nineteenth-century-looking costume by Vivienne Westwood. Nobody will accuse you of hypocrisy. In other words, the ecology trend may well be fulfilling one of our needs, but for the time being it is not succeeding in completely upsetting the fashion system.

One of the most important aspects of the ecology trend is 'naturalness' or 'back to nature'. What does this exactly entail? As I stated earlier, an era's ideals and desires are made visible in fashion. This is why every new fashion automatically provides the feeling that it is truer than the previous fashion. The new fashion style and the new look better match the new spirit of the times. Eighties fashion gave visual expression to a materialistic and achievement-oriented mentality. It was the era of assertiveness training, expensive design and big shiny cars. People wore clothes with broad shoulders made by expensive, well-known designers. Everything was focused on career, status and the corresponding outward show. By the nineties we had had enough of this egocentric possessiveness and the over-consumption that went with it. The new look is now called 'pure, authentic and natural' and has the pretension of being relaxed, unaffected and particularly timeless. We miss, however, the distance from our times to judge whether the 'naturalness' of the nineties is not just as artificial as the fashion styles of before. We can now smile at the seventies, for example, when heavy oak beams, handsome brickwork and a tiled floor served as a model for 'natural' country life. What this makes clear is that we should equally distrust the 'naturalness' of the nineties. In ten years time people will probably regard the current trend as just as artificial and arbitrary as the naturalism of the seventies.

Every 'back to nature' fashion clearly defines the points at which it is 'natural'. At the beginning of the twentieth century, Paul Poiret, influenced by the reform movement, introduced loose-hanging dresses that were meant to be worn without a corset. According to Poiret, this garment was much more natural since it followed the lines of the body. But suddenly very different demands were made of that 'natural' body. Instead of full and mature – the ideal of beauty until then – the ideal woman's body now had to be boyish, straight and flat. A clear sign that this body was not to be constricted in a corset. In order to achieve this 'boyish' result, voluptuous women had to resort to all sorts of new devices. They started to wear flatteners to press their unwanted bosom flat or they filled up too narrow waists so that the line of the body acquired the intended straight effect. It actually makes no difference whether a body is meant to express 'femininity', 'naturalness' or something else. Every fashion clearly indicates the methods by which this specific 'natural effect' can be obtained. Every ideal of beauty is clearly specified. Clothed or naked, a natural body does not exist. Everything bears traces of the times.

Leafing through current fashion magazines we stumble across products that are labeled 'natural', 'pure' or 'authentic'. Make-up, clothes and jewellery all suddenly have a connection with nature. In the October 1992 issue of the English *Vogue*, for example, we come across a fashion report called 'The Purists' featuring coats and sweaters whose colour is scarcely distinguishable from the dunes in the background. The accompanying text reads as follows: 'crossing a landscape where elegance meets the elements: in the foreground, smoothed

CLOTHES FOR THE LAND, ADVERTISEM

silhouettes and beachcombed (!) colours – from salt spray, to driftwood on suits and coats for the great outdoors.'

The insistent relationship between coats and sweaters and nature is not created by itself in this reportage. The fashion photograph may well evoke associations between the coats and the virgin dune landscape, but text is needed to indicate which details in the clothes this 'association with nature' actually applies to.[9] For when is a coat 'at one with the elements'? In this case – as we learn from the text – when the fabric is soft and the coat has a flowing form and a beige colour. By associating a few elements with nature, a fashion reportage can sophisticatedly transform an ordinary beige coat into a pure product of nature. The colour beige is particularly ideal as it can evoke all sorts of associations with ecological aspects, such as unbleached and eroded, driftwood and sand dunes, etc.

In this respect, it is enlightening to compare the French and English editions of *Vogue* from 1982/1983 with various *Vogues* from 1992/1993. Little has changed as regards aims. In the nineties the magazine was devoting just as much attention to luxury products like perfume, make-up and expensive jewellery, but the image that these products now have is vastly different from the image of ten years previously. The expensive necklaces in the November 1983 issue of the French *Vogue* are lavishly draped around champagne glasses held by glamorous women in gala clothing. This is no longer possible in the English *Vogue* of November 1992. The bracelets and necklaces are now draped around eels, oysters and other fish with the intention of emphasising their natural origin. Mutual similarities are used to enhance this image. The grey-blue colour of the pearls recurs in the colour of the fish and the form of a necklace fans out in the same 'natural' way as the fish tail on which the necklace is draped. The claws of the crab clasping a ring corresponds with the setting of the pearls. Even expensive and excessive jewels – the height of eighties ostentation – could thus be suddenly transformed into authentic natural treasures, 'Treasures From The Deep' that you can find on the seabed and that possess the same natural forms and colours as the fish in the darkness of the ocean.

Items of make-up are undergoing the same metamorphosis. Make-up too is now dominated by 'naturalness', with the result – paradoxically enough – that make-up techniques have become even more complicated than in the eighties. At that time make-up had to be distinctly visible. The guidelines of the 'nature trend' dictated that the body should make a healthy impression, that is to say, give the appearance of not being made up. The make-up of the nineties is so sophisticated that you have to guess what has been done to the face. Long, flashy red-painted nails are no longer fashionable, but nail care remains important. Nails are now short, filed roundly and finished off with transparent or mother-of-pearl polish so as to make a subtle, natural impression. Calvin Klein has his models appear on the catwalk with no make-up and photographs appear showing long, straight hair with no eye make-up or lipstick. The cheekbones and eyebrows, however, are accentuated so that the models look as though they are 'healthy' and wearing no make-up. In the English edition of *Vogue*, Sarah Mower describes this paradox of naturalness in the nineties as follows: 'Natural is as much a question of skill, artifice and fashion awareness as any other look. Get it wrong and by the standards of the time you won't look "natural" at all. Right now the nuances are in the brows and in a new sense of subtle shine.'

Even the sparse, Đcolourful' make-up that we are now seeing manages to skillfully establish a link with nature. Estée Lauder calls her new line with bright colours *Shades of the Rainforest*. The colours refer to the tropical hues of the jungle, the lustrous moistness of dew and the diffuse light shining through leaves. Dior makes an even more subtle connection. There the colours are no longer linked to elements from nature, but are seen as something emanating a magical and mystical effect. 'Colours enhance man's spiritual well-being', says Eliane Gouriou, the House of Dior's make-up expert. Nature in the form of primitive spiritual power.

An association with the spirit of the times is also sought in the case of fragrances. Perfumes nowadays are given a sober image linked to nature. President-director Maurice Roger of the House of Dior characterises his new *Dune* perfume as follows: '*Dune* is a reflection of our times. Dunes are the stable boundary between the world of flowers and plants and the ocean. A dune landscape is suffused with harmony, purity, peace and quiet, space: values that people are increasingly dreaming of since they are endangered values. We are feeling more and more oppressed in our materialistic world full of competitiveness, and in a physical sense our freedom of movement is also becoming smaller. Nature is being swallowed up by concrete.' This new philosophy is given visual support in the advertising campaign: what the photograph shows is not the usual glamorous lady, but a woman's face in the form of a hilly dune landscape from which the eyelashes rise up like a sprig of dune grass. A woman as dune landscape symbolising this fragrance of fresh, virgin nature.

The necessity - for in these times of ecological crisis do we still need expensive jewellery, clothes and make-up? - or the composition of a product makes no difference in the fashion system - it's first and foremost a question of new images. A whole new imaginary world can be created around any product by means of photographic images and captions. Coebergh blackcurrant gin effortlessly changed a few years ago from an old ladies' drink into an aphrodisiac for sensual and provocative young women. Even certain brands of coffee (such as Cafuego) are abandoning their classical image of domestic sociability for an exciting aura. The nature/purity trend in fashion is also applicable to many products in the same way, without the content of the product having anything to do with natural or ecological processes. 'Back to nature' is little more than yet another fashion

ESPRIT, ECOLLECTI

trend that will be replaced within a few years by the next dream.

Diametrically opposed to the visual deception of the 'back to nature' or eco-trend is the ecology movement in the proper sense of the word: producers and designers who are actually making clothing on the basis of an environmentally-aware perspective. They do not believe in the simple and, in the meantime, self-evident translation of a spirit of the age into a visual theme, but rather concern themselves with the entire life cycle of the product. They search for alternative materials, for dye baths and methods of production that do as little harm to nature as possible. Esprit, Body Shop and Levi's are just a few examples of major companies that are working on ecologically responsible clothing products. So as not to fall into the trap of the eco-look, Esprit in particular has developed a distinguishing strategy to draw attention to these ecological products or ecological views.

For the past two seasons Esprit has an 'environmentally-friendly' clothing collection, the so-called Eco-collection. It has been presenting these collections first of all as an experimental production line for trying out environmentally-friendly techniques. One of the things that Esprit has done is to experiment with tweed made from second-hand clothes. If it turns out that the eco techniques function so well that they can be used in large-scale production, they will also be applied at a later stage to the production of the regular collection. The Eco-collection is expressly not being presented as a separate Esprit trend or theme. Visual information is less important than the story behind it, so the clothes are not given a particular visual image. The press and the public have to be satisfied with photographs of details such as handmade buttons or buttonhole stitches. Esprit's usual total image, primarily focusing on a certain type of person, is lacking. This time Esprit provides extensive information about the way these collections come into being. The buttons are made according to an ancient technique in Ghana, where local craftsmen pulverise old bottles and then add pigment to smelt them into colourful buttons. 'Can buttons on clothes mean more than a fashion expression?' is the question posed in Esprit's press release. The answer is, 'Certainly, you can provide people living in areas with low employment with extra income. And they can preserve crafts.'[10] Esprit's presentation thus shifts attention from a visual image to a text concerning content. The interesting thing is that it is not the eco product itself that is important, but Esprit's environmentally-conscious attitude towards clothing and the Third World. In other words, the eco-collection is not presented as an aesthetic image, but as an ethical product. Esprit is hence implicitly promoting its honest business practices and that interest transcends any look or fashion style. The message is: Esprit is ideologically correct so you should shop for clothes in their store.

Luciano Benetton was already selling clothes on the basis of this strategy a few years earlier. 'Fashion styles and products change so fast that a company

AMERICAN APPAREL,
ADVERTISEMENT

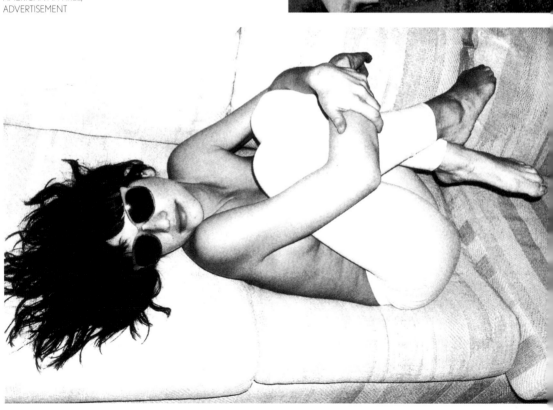

VEXED GENERATION, *NINJA FLEECE*, AUTUMN/WINTER 1995/1996

ESPRIT, ECOLLECTION, AUTUMN/WINTER 1992

PATAGONIA, FLEECE JACKET AND ORGANIC COTTON T-SHIRT, SPRING/ SUMMER 1996

image is the only thing that can remain constant; it makes no sense to have a product image', says Benetton. This is why Benetton's advertisements display 'a new style of ethics and engagement'. A range of differently coloured children serves as a pamphlet against racism, a duck covered in oil raises the issue of the environment. In one of the campaigns Luciano shows himself to be ecologically conscious by appearing totally naked in the photograph behind a slogan calling for the collection of old clothes. Mexx has found it difficult to hold its ground within all these ecological principles. It introduced what is certainly a very bizarre variant of these new advertising images: a photograph showing a bathtub in the jungle in which a naked black man is making love to a likewise naked but white woman. The idea seems to be that Mexx wants to be seen as a company that is in favour of anti-racial eco-sex.

Esprit and Benetton, then, are disconnecting product, message and image. The message is no longer cloaked in an image around a product, but is conveyed in a company mentality that functions and is conveyed independently of the products. The appearance and aesthetics of the product have not become unimportant, of course, but they are made secondary. Clothes are no longer to be seen in advertisements, but only in the shop itself. The company is thus selling itself primarily on the basis of conscientious ideas, its ethics. And not on the basis of an 'aesthetic' style as fashion houses and fashion designers previously did and in most cases still continue to do.

The Body Shop, a worldwide chain of skin care products, works on the basis of the same philosophy as Esprit, except that it does not advertise. Founder and director Anita Roddick finds the existing images surrounding make-up and skin care discriminating. 'We're still seeing mainly white, beautiful and super slim women and these have little to do with everyday reality.' An interesting argument as the whole idea behind make-up is based on an attempt at transcending everyday reality and physical 'defects'. But for the Body Shop it was a reason to ignore visual imagery, except when it had to do with the furnishing of the shop and how the pots and bottles looked. The main thing is the organic and environmentally-friendly composition of the product. Products are not tested on animals and the Body Shop only uses ingredients that are biodegradable. Care is taken that the packaging is recyclable – in each of its shops bottles can be refilled. The Body Shop 'philosophy' is mainly focused on the intimate pleasure that can be experienced from the product. Nowhere is there a promise of the magic of eternal youth or an overwhelming sensuality. The Body Shop has proved in recent years that consumers can also become interested in a product without these visual dreams. In only twenty years and without a single advertising campaign the Body Shop grew into a company quoted on the stock market. Consumers appreciate its 'honest', unadorned products and its caring attitude towards the world. The Body Shop uses its profits to support all sorts of initiatives. In every shop there are folders, photographs and videos displaying projects, including several in the Third World, that have been initiated by the Body Shop. So when the consumer throws the Brazilian bath pearl costing one guilder into her bath, she knows that a percentage of that guilder will end up with an Amazonian tribe in the Brazilian rainforest. The Brazilian bath pearl does not represent any classical desire for beauty, it does not promise the purchaser a new identity, no magical exterior, but it does capitalise on ethical sensibilities and gives the consumer the pleasant feeling that she is also behaving in a socially correct way when taking a bath. The consumer has undergone a metamorphosis – from a vain, wasteful purchaser to a benefactor who not only contributes to a better environment, but also to a better society. Esprit and the Body Shop have thus abandoned a visual product image, replacing it with a new, ostensible sincerity. Big companies like these try to reduce the exploitation of the environment by using closed dye baths and organically cultivated cotton. And they strive for a more 'sustainable' system of production. Esprit, for example, is stimulating coca farmers in Columbia to switch to cotton cultivation by offering higher prices for cotton than for coca leaves. But ultimately such an approach does nothing to change the Third World's dependency on its status as a source of cheap labour. The fashion system as a capitalist undertaking remains intact. Intentions may improve, but the classic goal of these companies – to become bigger and make more profit – is never called into question. 'Caring Capitalism', as Roddick terms her own business politics, is essentially no different from classical nineteenth-century charity campaigns which were more about redeeming one's own guilt feelings about the unjust distribution of wealth and power than about actually changing things. The company politics of Esprit, Body Shop and Benetton are sops to the conscience. Anita Roddick's trips to the Third World, constantly captured on video and in series of photographs, are moreover very much like modern missionary expeditions. Roddick as a missionary demonstratively displaying her charity and generosity to the world in order to delude the consumer of her products into believing that she (and thus the consumer too) wishes the world and the environment the best. In this way the consumer's eyes are reassuringly closed. Caring Capitalism.

Ecological ideas have also influenced avant-garde fashion designers like Martin Margiela, Jean Colonna and Xuly Bet, as well as street styles like Grunge, resulting in a new mentality as regards fashion. Rather than focus on ecological production, they are resisting fashion's obsession with innovation and concentrating once again on the cut and the material. The Dutch fashion label Orson & Bodil even sees the search for new images as meaningless: ÐMost items of clothing have already acquired their ideal proportions and appearance over the course of time. New is therefore no longer interesting in this day and age, as there's hardly anything new to be invented.' This new fashion mentality was reflected in October 1992 in a slide presentation at Première Vision in Paris, the first and most important fabric fair of the season: the designer was depicted as a surgeon taking apart the construction of a sleeve opening. What this made clear was that the new type of fashion designer no longer focuses attention on a new image or exterior, but on the interior. This line of approach is elaborated in various ways by different designers. Martin Margiela and Xuly Bet, for example, mainly draw their inspiration from secondhand clothing. Martin Margiela studies labourers' jackets in order to analyse and imitate their comfortable fit. He incorporates all sorts of extra seams in the sleeve so as to give the jacket the maximum span and freedom of movement. In the October 1992 issue of *The Face*, Joe Casely Hayford described the new clothing habits of English youth and young designers whom he met while giving guest lectures in Belgium and the Netherlands. He refers to them as Bovril Babes, as though to suggest an appearance from which soup could be made. He sees the Bovril Babes as fitting in the tradition of Demeulemeester and Margiela. In their case it is a question of an original combination of beautifully made designer clothes with secondhand and inexpensive ready-to-wear garments: a wraparound skirt made from a flannel bed sheet with a leather jacket by Helmut Lang worn over a C&A sweater. The motto is always that the 'right look' can no longer be acquired through status, money or a designer label inside the collar, but through independently creating an original combination. Ready-made design is cheap, a self-constructed style is chic.

Although designers like Orson & Bodil and Yohji Yamamoto do not work with secondhand clothing, they do draw inspiration from the traditional tailoring designs that they mainly find in men's clothing from earlier periods. In a documentary by Wim Wenders, Yamamoto revealed his fascination for August Sander's photographs depicting the clothes worn by various professional groups at the time of the Weimar Republic and how they inspired him to imbue his designs in advance with the worn quality that these clothes displayed – the typical folds of the jacket around the sleeves and the rolling form of a worn shirt.

Orson & Bodil also find the sensory pleasures and comfort of a well-cut garment extremely important. A few seasons ago they made a waistcoat with pockets lined with different fabrics – one with cotton, the other with silk, a third with thick, soft felt. Only the wearer derives any pleasure from this – others simply don't see it. In this way the chicness of the nineties rises to the surface once again. You no longer wear clothes in order to impress others, but purely for your own pleasure, since they offer all sorts of sensual, personal pleasures. Fashion thus changes from an exhibitionistic pleasure into an autistic one. People no longer talk about fashion, but about clothes. The most important thing is not the exterior, but the sensual and intrinsic values of clothes. The exterior is assimilated through being inconspicuous – barely any colour and simple, sober forms. Only those elements that refer to comfort may be accentuated. In the case of Orson & Bodil this could be a particularly beautiful cut or treating the fabric in such a way that its materiality is done optimum justice to.

Ecological notions of authenticity and naturalness are given a new interpretation here. They no longer have to do just with an image, but with tangible, concrete emotions. Such clothing stimulates our body, becoming an experience that comes closer to ourselves. And that gives us a feeling of authenticity and sincerity that is of a different order than the previously mentioned beige coat with the colour of bleached driftwood.

Do these new developments mean that the fashion system has fundamentally changed in the nineties? Probably not, since regressive movements that give a different interpretation to the fashion system – as we see happening now – are nothing new. Youth culture in the sixties and seventies undermined the monopoly of the established fashion houses in Paris and demonstrated that, in addition to a prescribed fashion, there was also something like a fashion of the street. A fashion that had little to do with status and prestige, but was certainly suitable for displaying alternative ideas. From then on and for the first time, fashion could no longer be seen as that one absolute style or length of skirt, but as embracing several themes, styles and ideas simultaneously.

While counter-movements from the street simply continued, designers experienced a revival in the eighties. Together with Vivienne Westwood, Jean Paul Gaultier was the best interpreter of post-modernism in fashion. He cheerfully mixed all sorts of styles from the history of fashion, his most important goal being to completely jumble up habitual standards and values concerning what makes clothing beautiful, ugly, chic or shabby, and to call into question the function of an item of clothing. He combined jogging pants with spangled evening wear, adulterated a handbag by attaching a dog's lead to it, used a shower hose as a belt and made parkas from organza. In this way Gaultier removed clothing and fabrics from their classical context, stripping them of their original connotations. The expectations and cultural codes of items of clothing were thus questioned in the eighties.[11] And now, in the nineties we have ended up almost as a matter of course with what is still left over: the item of clothing itself. Fashion was always focused on the exterior and the image, but it is now turning inward or is becoming spiritualised, as clothing is experienced in the form of sensitivity and ethics. A new point of view concerning fashion is thus being created, one that perfectly matches the reflective, introverted attitude already associated with the nineties. In an age when communication and human contact are becoming redundant because of homeshopping, online banking and holiday excursions into Virtual Reality via the home computer, this same autism is also reflected in all manner of cultural manifestations. In brain machines that enable one to be amused in isolation, as well as in clothing that is mainly intended for giving pleasure to the individual self.

Jean Baudrillard proposed two decades ago that fashion has a permanent urge to renew its signs, generating an infinite production of signifiers. It plays a game with change, with all signifiers being constantly subject to new combinations and brought up for discussion. In recent decades it is no longer a question of stylistic variations and forms, but of the codings and expectations vis-à-vis clothing. Nothing has in fact changed with regard to the system of fashion. Fashion, after all, continues to simultaneously fulfil the need for innovation and on the other hand the need to leave the existing order unchanged.[12]

---

1   RISC (Research Institute on Social Change) is an international research office that was commissioned by DuPont to look into consumer behaviour in the nineties. RISC conducts annual research in the seventeen most important industrialised countries and has been interviewing the same groups for years (30,000 persons per year). It tests the findings of its questionnaires against media and semiotic research. In December 1992 the report was presented to the Dutch press by the Netherlands Media Institute during the Triumph fashion show.

2   Goos Geursen, *Tijdens de verkoop gaat de verbouwing gewoon door*. Leiden (Stenfert Kroese) 1992. Faith Popcorn, *The Popcorn Report*. New York (Doubleday) 1991.

3   Sebastien de Diesbach, director of the trend office Promostyl, describes it in powerful terms: the twenty-first century is ecological or else it will no longer exist.

4   Roland Barthes, *Système de la mode*. Paris (Seuil) 1967.

5   Philippe Perrot, *Le travail des apparences*. Paris (Seuil) 1984.

6   Philippe Perrot, *op. cit.*

7   'They testify to a dream of wholeness, according to which the human being is everything at once and does not have to choose.' Roland Barthes, 'The Rhetoric of the Signifier', *Versus*, 4 (1985), p. 49.

8   'Fashion is a system of signs that naturalises the arbitrary. It's aim is to make absurd and meaningless changes look "natural". Roland Barthes, *Système de la mode*.

9   'And fashion not only protects us from reminders of decay; it is also a mirror held up to fix the shaky boundaries of the psychological self. It glazes the shifty identity, freezing it into the certainty of image.' Elizabeth Wilson, *Adorned in Dreams*. London (Virago Press) 1985, pp. 58-59.

10 Esprit press release, November 1992.

11 Marylène Delbourg-Delphis, *La mode pour la vie*. Paris 1983.

12 Jean Baudrillard, *L'échange symbolique et la mort*. Paris (Gallimard) 1976, p. 141.

KARIM BENAMMAR

40

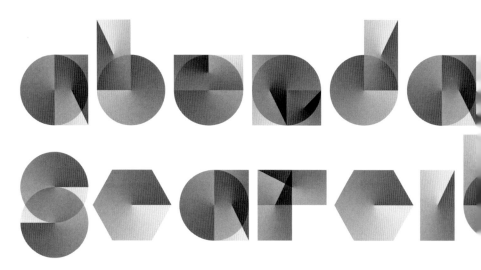

CONCEPTS AND RHETORIC
IN ECOLOGY, ECONOMICS,
AND ECO-ETHICS

The notions of abundance and scarcity lie at the heart of the current debate between those in business and most economists on one side, and the growing number of those concerned with the ecological fate of the earth on the other.

We are, by any account, more materially wealthy than at any other time in history; even the middle classes can afford a level of affluence that was the preserve of kings not so long ago. The increases in technology and communication have made life extremely comfortable. Stock markets are booming, and suddenly everyone is talking about stocks, bonds, portfolios, following the markets more than they are following the weather. American economists speak confidently of a new era of continuing growth fueled by technological developments, where the periodic contractions of the market can be avoided. The neo-liberalist school of free-market economics paints a rosy picture of ever-increasing affluence produced by developments in technology, combined with the liberalization of global commerce.

There is a sense of material abundance: we have ever-increasing material possessions, ever more choices and amounts of food, ever more world travel, instant world-wide communications, indeed we have ever-expanding horizons on all sides. There is economic abundance; material things abound; there is plenty, a sense of richness and well-being. This ever-expanding economic abundance is predicated on continuing growth, on the continuing extraction of resources, the continuing manufacture of consumer items spurred by new technological developments, and the continuing liberalization of world-trade in removing the last obstacles to a global economy.[1]

Against this sense of plenty and ever-expanding horizons, the main thrust of the ecological consciousness movement that has been growing over the last few decades has been the elaboration of the need for a limit to our runaway consumption and production of waste. Those in the ecological movement argue for a natural boundary: our resources are not unlimited, and there are unexpected limits of which we have only recently become aware. Our worry about the oil reserves left in the world has been supplanted by a different limit and a different worry; even if we have plenty of oil left, we cannot burn it all since it will contribute too much to global warming.

A consensus is emerging that we cannot maintain this rate of depletion of natural resources. The main point is that the resources we have for so long considered to be limitless and free, such as clean air, clean water and a temperate climate, are in fact not unlimited; we are running up against the limits of the carrying capacity of the planetary eco-system. There is still some argument as to what precisely these limits are: while early doomsday scenarios of Malthusians in the sixties and seventies focused on population growth, the population has not risen as fast as projected and the carrying capacity of the earth has increased dramatically.

This is in essence the point of contention between the cornucopians and those who see limits to our growth.[2] A cornucopian like Julian Simon argues that human ingenuity, technology, and economic development have and always will provide a solution to any environmental or resource challenge. For example, the problem of having more mouths to feed will be solved by the development of genetically engineered crops with a higher yield, or crops which grow in desert conditions. The energy crisis will be solved by increased efficiency, making nuclear energy safe, or perhaps by an unknown factor such as a breakthrough in fusion research. The human capacity for adapting and carrying on has always been greater than the crises that have faced us. One of the merits of Simon's argument is that it shows us that we have more than a static set of tools to face any coming challenges.

The other camp, represented here by Norman Myers, argues that there are inherent limits to the earth's carrying capacity, that there are certain thresholds which we are overstepping right at this moment. Our material development has a deleterious effect on other species; species are vanishing at a faster rate now than ever through loss of habitat and pollution. Our exponential growth patterns are coming up against some clear and unshakable limits: with both our population and standard of living set to double in the next forty years, we will clearly be facing some momentous breakdown before then if we continue at present rates of extraction and consumption. Even at our present consumption levels, there is hardly any space left for other forms of life.

The problem, of course, is compounded by the fact that many of these environmental problems are long-term processes the effects of which we are just beginning to feel but the results of which will be catastrophic: the erosion of topsoil in the world's richest agricultural areas, the depletion of aquifers, the buildup of crud and silt, the depletion of fisheries, and long-term pollution problems such as dioxin finding its way through the food chain. Mother's milk is so toxic in some countries that it would not pass food safety standards. These problems have long incubation periods and are cumulative – a point of no-return will be reached. According to many scientists, the point where irreparable damage has been done has already come and gone; the question now is how much we can cushion and repair this damage.

The argument from the ecological camp, then, is one of scarcity, of a lack of limitless natural resources. The French philosopher Michel Serres puts it succinctly: 'The Earth cannot give to all its children that which the rich wrest from it today. There is scarcity.'[3] In opposition to the material abundance of the neoliberal free-traders, the ecological camp stresses the fact that the planetary ecosystem has limited resources which are fast being depleted. According to the Gaia thesis, the earth itself is a living organism which can only support so much use and abuse. There is not enough clean air and clean water and space at the present ever-increasing levels of consumption for all of us, although there may be enough for some of us. Indeed we find that the wealth of the richest group of people on earth is also exponentially increasing.[4] Unless there is a pretty drastic change in our consumption patterns, style and method, we are headed towards environmental ruin.

The battle-lines seem to be drawn between economic abundance and ecological scarcity. Of course both the word 'economics' and 'ecology' hearken back to the *oikos*, the living space or habitat, to our home and environment as individuals, communities, and species - the *nomos* of the *oikos* and the *logos* of the *oikos*. Although these words in their common English usage are rather far removed from their etymology, it is still worth pointing out the close kinship between the two. The *nomos* of the *oikos* is concerned with the distribution of resources and wealth, and the structure of that distribution, the regulation of the flow of wealth within the *oikos*. There is also a *logos* to the *oikos*: ecology consists in considering the discourse and logic of the earth itself, which is rather different from the regulation of the *nomos*. Ecological thinking considers the *logos* of the *oikos* itself, not considered merely from the point of view of its *nomos*-use, its economic use.

Against the abundance of economics and technological innovation, against the bounty in comfort and material wealth, then, we find an ecological notion of scarcity. Several concepts of limit have been put forward: Ivan Illich talks about a sense of discipline in our usage and consumption, or *askesis*. *Askesis* means taking less than we need and using less than we need: our wants and desires are subordinated to an ecologically sustainable supply of goods. Michel Serres proposes the notion of self-restraint: 'Reason puts aside some reason to restrain itself.'[5] We can take more but we should restrain ourselves from doing so, even and especially when it lies within our power do so: 'To enjoy power and not take advantage of it is the beginning of wisdom, of civilization.'[6]

Against the concept of economic abundance, of free trade, open markets, the information super-highway, of everyone getting into stocks, and of the ever-quickening pace of the use of energy, resources, money, and innovation, we find an ecological sense of self-restraint, of self-imposed limits, or of *askesis*.

But perhaps things are not as they seem. The problem lies not with the use of the concepts of abundance and scarcity, but with the rhetoric of abundance. Indeed, the rhetoric of material abundance is a flawed rhetoric, and one which pushes the ecological camp into a position of arguing for a notion of scarcity. The problem lies with the nature of our present economic system. The problem is no longer the technological system - whereas it used to be technology versus the environment, it has now become economics versus the environment. Scientific research itself has had to become economically viable, and technological development is also subordinate to economic constraints. Although Microsoft gets praised as an example of technological innovation, its success is actually based on the clever and merciless marketing of a technologically inferior product. The bottom line of the free market is where we are all headed to: local governments and governmental agencies, community services and university department as well as companies have to become efficient in the pursuit of high and quick returns on investment.

But the fundamental concept of economics is scarcity: a thing has value in terms of its scarcity: the price of diamonds, gold, oil or coffee is set according to their relative scarcity, real or anticipated. Clean air and clean water were until very recently without any economic value, and it is still very difficult to factor in environmental values into economic calculations.[7] This scarcity of goods can be artificially maintained through monopolistic or proprietary practices, or, as in the case of the price of oil in the early nineties, an abundance of cheap goods can be defended in the Gulf by 'politics by other means'. Another look at our so-called abundant materiality reveals scarcity gone wild. Scarcity lies at the basis of economic theory; it supports the economic structure and fuels the engine of economic growth. Advertising, which ceaselessly encourages economic consumption and therefore economic growth, is a response to a lack, a scarcity within us, a deep-felt psychological need for reassurance through consumption. We are not cool unless we have a new sporty automobile; our fragile egos are strengthened by the latest perfumes and brand-name fashion, and new computer gadgets keep us occupied. There is a constant appeal to needs within us, to the hungry ghosts whose hunger can never be appeased.

Moreover, the globalization of the free-market economy exports this concept and experience of scarcity to the so-called Third World, exports this sense of scarcity to societies and cultures where this sense of scarcity never existed, where there was no concept of consumer economics and ever-increasing growth rates. The lack and need represented by this feeling of scarcity lies in a very human character trait: *greed*. The booming stock market of the last few years is testimony to the allure of greed; portfolios advertise with annual returns of forty percent on investment through dubious and risky manipulations, as if an annual return on investment of forty percent is something any business could produce for any length of time. We are addicted to the continuous growth and expansion of our economies, to the ever-expanding production of consumer goods and the concomitant production of waste.

My central point here is to argue that the rhetoric of material abundance masks the fact that the fundamental concept of economics is in reality scarcity. Conversely, although ecologists, confronted with the rhetoric of material abundance, have been forced to argue for a concept of scarcity and self-restraint, the fundamental concept of the *logos* of our *oikos*, of life on earth, is abundance.

Abundance, from the Latin *ab-unda*, from the water, the wave, that which over-flows, is the sense of bounty, of plenty, the sense of living things and life itself which flowers and grows. The luxurious growth of the natural forest, the inherent goodness of air and water, the fullness of the harvest (we say: an abundant year), the bounty of vegetable and animal life are indeed the *logos* of our *oikos*.

We can simply put it in terms of 'scarcity thinking' versus 'abundance think-ing'. Scarcity thinking is linked to fear and unfulfilled needs; abundance thinking is a sense of plenty in life, a sense of the bounty of living. Perhaps this distinction can be illustrated through the philosophical discussion of the gift.[8] In one sense, a gift is an exchange; when it comes down to it, a gift is always exchanged for something else, and complex systems of mutual gift-giving have evolved in dif-ferent societies and different cultures. But the notion of exchange is already an economic notion, pointing to the beginning of trade: I give something but I get something else for it in return. A gift in this sense of exchange, in this economic sense, partakes not of the notion of abundance but rather of that of scarcity; the gift is in a way conditional upon the expected return on one's investment. Can we then not conceive of the generosity of a gift given without expectation of return, conceive of a true gift rather than an investment?

'Gift' means not only a 'present', but also a 'talent', as when we speak of a gifted person. There are musical, artistic, even commercial gifts. In this sense, a gift is given without expectation of a return. Our talents are given, even if they have to be developed through practice. Life itself, in a spiritual sense, is a con-tinuous giving without thought of return. The sun is burning itself out without thought or sense of return. Plant life is ceaselessly growing, giving of its bounty without thought or sense of return. And we, as human beings, are gifts without return – what on earth would a return on a life lived to the full be, or an invest-ment return on the unfolding of a life understood and lived as a gift? Life, in its essence, is not a return for something else. It is this sense of gift, generosity and abundance without return which does not fall under the rhetoric of exchange. Moreover, some values do not partake of economic exchange: indeed, for some values, the more one gives, the more receives, and the more one produces in turn. This is the fundamental quality of love in all its various guises, such as trust, or care, or friendship.

Distinct from economics and ecology, eco-ethics is concerned with the *ethos* of the *oikos*, with the human sense of the good to be found in the *oikos* in which we dwell. In other words, a moral sense of what it means to be human beings living on earth. Eco-ethics can provide a study of the value and concepts involved in the rhetoric of abundance, the rhetorical game which puts ecologi-cal thinking on the defensive, and can help us distinguish an appeal to the base human instinct of greed from a more spiritual sense of being human. Human beings, as a life-form, are naturally generous, abundant in their being.

The 'celebration' of material and economic abundance is nothing but a celebration of human greed, of scarcity, of human pain, human fear, and unchecked human desire. Economic thinking projects these human values onto the *oikos*, onto the practice of the world stage. A celebration of natural abundance, on the other hand, is a celebration on many levels: on the level of nature, on the level of the world, the *oikos*; a celebration of the gifts that we are as human beings (we are all the same in that we are all unique). It is a celebration of the chance to develop our talents, to bring them to fruition, to give through the exercise of our gifts, to be of service. A celebration, then, of the spiritual aspirations of human beings; as the Italian philosopher Marco Olivetti tells us, becoming human is what is calling us, what we are working toward; it is not our starting point.[9] Becoming human is something worth striving toward, which is realized through our life.

This reversal in the attribution of the concepts of abundance and scarcity is not merely a correction of a rhetorical ploy. The nature of the argument from the ecological side changes. Even though many of the practical proposals put forward by ecological thinkers for a sustainable world, from energy taxes to alternative manufacturing practices to a rediscovery of the local, would remain the same, there is a crucial shift in emphasis. It is the difference between arguing for *enough* and for *plenty*; although these words are close in meaning, their connotations are rather different: 'just enough' suggests that we are barely scraping by, that there is a voluntary or an involuntary restriction on our use, consumption, or enjoyment. Plenty, on the other hand, is a synonym of abundance, of bounty: to have plenty is to have 'more than enough', 'more than one needs', plenty to enjoy, use or consume. Enough and plenty can refer to the same amount of goods or energy usage: the crucial difference is one of *attitude*, the difference between coming from a position of scarcity and coming from a position of abundance.

The abundance inherent in life and nature is something which human beings can only partially glimpse, experience or comprehend. Our senses have to filter out most levels of experience to get by in the practical world. The overflow of experience cannot be exhaustively mined; there is a constant overflow of energy, of giving, of joy which we cannot all take in at the same time. We are the ones who limit our attention to the world, our attunement to it, and sometimes seek artificial realities.

Another way of defining the concept of natural abundance I wish to develop here comes from examining the concept of excess. To exceed is to go over the limits of the rational, the reasonable, the socially or morally appropriate. Transcending, exceeding, going beyond a certain limit. Our present consumption patterns and the production of waste are excessive in this way: every single person in the industrialized world directly or indirectly produces 15,000 kilos, or approximately 200 times their own weight, in waste products every year.[10]

Some of these waste products are so toxic to life-forms that they cannot be recycled in any way in the production process. This is the sense of excessive consumption, excessive production, excessive deforestation and depletion of natural resources, excessive remuneration for the world's richest group. But there is also a different sense of excess, the excess of energy in life which is produced beyond what is necessary to maintain the organism and for reproductive purposes, the excess of art, of the erotic, of the carnival.[11] The Balinese, like most 'traditional' cultures, were not engaged in an economy geared to ever-increasing production. Balinese used to work only a few weeks a year on their island of plenty, to communally plant and harvest the rice. Most of their time was what we now perversely call 'free' time, and they gave themselves over to the development of their talents through the gifts of painting, music, dance, and festivals. What are Mendelssohn's 'Italian' Symphony or Beethoven's *Ode to Joy*, Picasso's paintings, Alvin Ailey's choreographies, Walt Whitman and Rumi's poetry but celebrations of excess, of abundance, of bounty? Of the excess energies of being human, the excess energies of being alive?

We respond to the abundant calling of the world and of our fellow human beings, not by restricting our energy, by limiting our responses, by being stingy with our knowledge, abilities, talents, attention, but by celebrating the abundance of life through the excess of our presence.

Our attunement to the *ethos* of the *oikos*, to its *logos* and its *nomos*, has shown us the concept of abundance in life and human beings and its co-optation by the rhetoric of economic growth. But by externalizing our abundant sense of life in ever-more rapid and brutal consumption and waste production, we are not celebrating a very progressive side of our nature. Rather, we are projecting our deep animal fears of insecurity, fear, lack, want, and scarcity on a global scale through rampant consumerism. We are shutting out most of that which is glorious, joyous and bountiful about us by interpreting it narrowly as economic production, and by this action threatening our own survival. We are busying ourselves with the business of replacing the diversity of plants and species and of our own local cultures and modes of being with a global monoculture of greed tethered to an economic bottom line which is as nonsensical as it is perverse.

In the end, though, it is not a question of 'us' versus 'them', not a fight to the death between the businessman and the ecologist, between the *nomos* and the *logos* of our *oikos*. The cornucopia envisioned by Simon is also an expression of the unbridled creativity of the human spirit, scientific and technological progress an outcome of our natural curiosity; economic exchange is a cornerstone of the creation of community and communal and cultural identity. Some of the strongest critics of the way corporations destroy our natural and ethical environment, such as Paul Hawken, Joshua Karliner, and David Korten, also agree that it is not

48

business as such which is the problem but rather the widespread externalization of environmental and social costs by companies.[12] This externalization of costs means that we are paying far less than the real cost of goods, the balance being made up by exploited workers and the plunder of non-renewable resources. Companies are forced to externalize as many costs as possible by the present financial system in which vast sums of invested money are scouring the globe for the best short-term return possible regardless of consequences.

Despite the rhetoric of material abundance celebrated by our daily dose of advertising, there is in truth nothing abundant about depleting the natural and human resources of a bountiful planet in the fastest way possible. Rather, it is a deep sense of insecurity, fear and scarcity thinking which pushes us to grab as much as possible of the available resources before they run out, and this way of acting, like all pathologies, becomes a self-fulfilling prophecy. It is the scarcity thinking of economic theory which posits a world of limited goods and pleasures for which there is unequal competition. In a truly abundant world, re-sources are husbanded, there is no waste since all by-products are an integral part of the cycle, and the sense of plenty, of bountiful living is an expression of the knowledge that there is always more for those who come after us, that, as a celebration of the gifts we are as human beings, we always give more than we take, out of human generosity, out of our gratitude for being alive.

1   See William Greider, *One World, Ready or Not. The Manic Logic of Global Capitalism*. New York (Simon and Schuster) 1997.

2   Norman Myers and Julian L. Simon, *Scarcity or Abundance? A Debate on the Environment*. New York (W.W. Norton) 1994.

3   Michel Serres, *Le tiers instruit*. Paris (François Bourin) 1991, p. 192.

4   The 358 billionaires in the world in 1994 owned as much wealth as the 2.5 billion people at the bottom of the pile. David C. Korten, *When Corporations Rule the World*. West Hartford, Conn. (Kumarian Press) 1995, p. 83.

5   Michel Serres, *op.cit.*, p. 184. Serres also applies this notion of self-restraint to our use of knowledge and our scientific curiosity.

6   Michel Serres, *op.cit*, p. 192.

7   The integration of environmental costs in economic calculations is a major aim of the ecological movement. For example, Norman Myers and Julian L. Simon, *op.cit.*, pp. 97-99. For a perspective from the business community, see Stephan Schmidtheiny *et al.*, *Financing Change. The Financial Community, Eco-efficiency, and Sustainable Development*. Cambridge, Mass. (mit Press) 1998.

8   See the articles in Alan D. Schrift (ed.), *The Logic of the Gift*. New York (Routledge) 1997.

9   Comments made during the discussion of his paper at the *Seventeenth Taniguchi Symposium*; see Marco M. Olivetti, 'Incarnation of the Ought', in *Acta Intitutionis Philosophiae et Aestheticae*, xviii (1997), pp. 155-164.

10 Figure extrapolated from Paul Hawken, *The Ecology of Commerce*. New York (Harper Collins) 1993, p. 37.

11 See Alphonso Lingis, *Excesses. Eros and Culture*. Albany (State University of New York Press) 1984.

12 Paul Hawken, *op.cit.*; David C. Korten, *op.cit.*; Joshua Karliner, *The Corporate Planet. Ecology and Politics in the Age of Globalization*. San Francisco (Sierra Club Books) 1997, pp. 38-9.

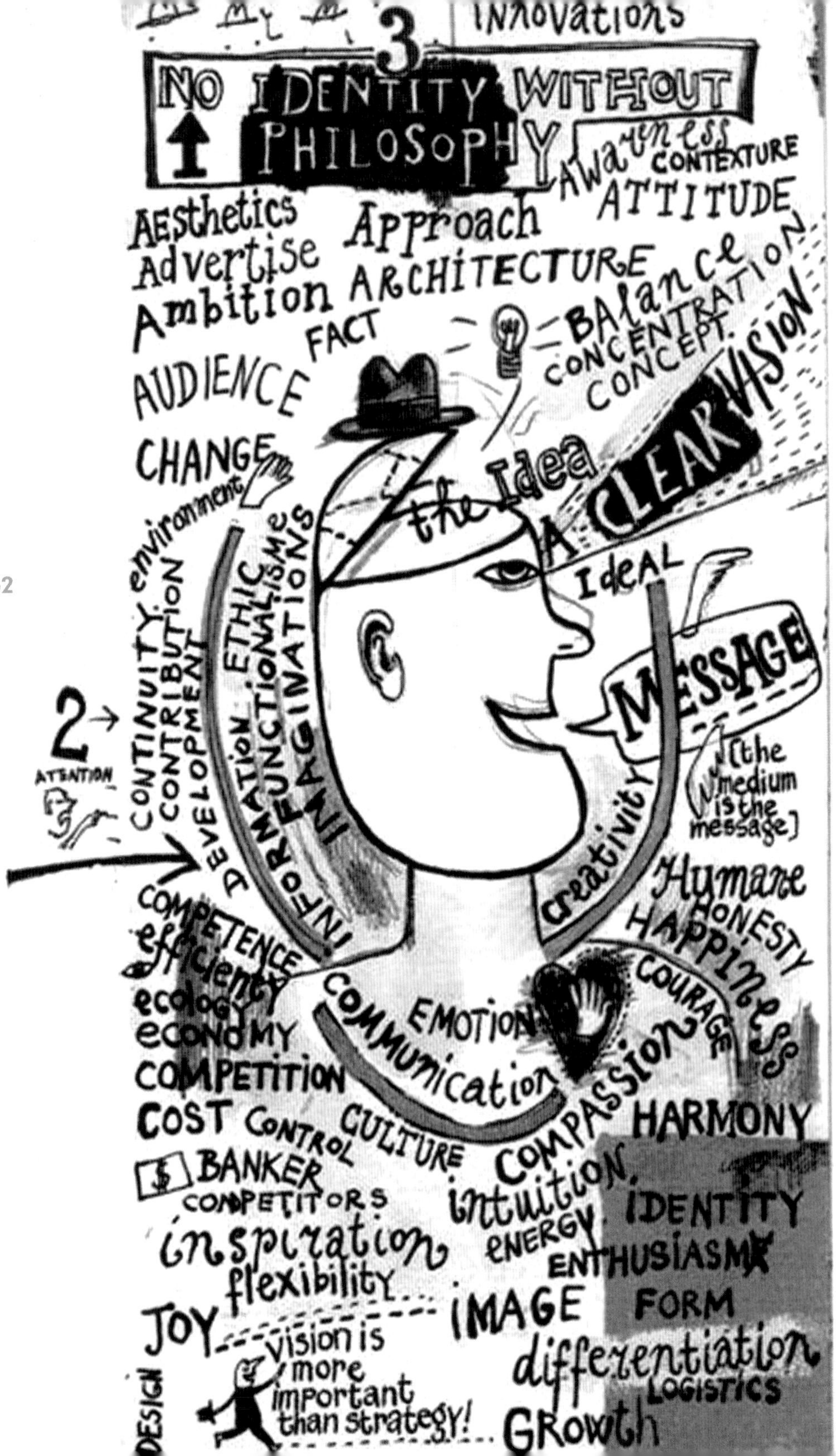

3

NO IDENTITY WITHOUT PHILOSOPHY

↑

INNOVATIONS

Awareness CONTEXTURE

Aesthetics Approach ATTITUDE
Advertise
Ambition ARCHITECTURE
FACT BALANCE
AUDIENCE CONCENTRATION
CONCEPT
CHANGE VISION

environment the Idea A CLEAR

CONTINUITY
CONTRIBUTION IDEAL
DEVELOPMENT MESSAGE
INFORMATION ETHIC FUNCTIONALISME
IMAGINATIONS [the medium is the message]

2 →
ATTENTION

creativity
Humane
HONESTY
HAPPINESS
COMPETENCE COURAGE
efficiency
ecology EMOTION
economy COMMUNICATION COMPASSION
COMPETITION intuition HARMONY
COST CONTROL CULTURE energy IDENTITY
$ BANKER ENTHUSIASM
COMPETITORS IMAGE FORM
inspiration
flexibility differentiation
JOY LOGISTICS
vision is GROWTH
DESIGN more
important
than strategy!

52

AN TEUNEN

shaping society by design

Indefatigable production and designing, globalisation, the unilateral subjection of life as a whole to the economy and the obsession with progress – these phenomena have led to so much alienation, imbalance, uncertainty and destruction that producers, consumers and designers are starting to have second thoughts. Companies, also in the fashion branch, have to broaden their attitude towards products and markets and orient themselves more emphatically towards society. Fashion houses should become paragons of frugality and environmental protection, as well as of solidarity and cultural practice. If fashion companies want to achieve the necessary inner harmony, then all stakeholders ought to display involvement. Designers should fulfil a pioneering role in this. The very nature of their profession means that their work should serve others and it is precisely they who should devote themselves to the design of society. Unfortunately many fashion designers have to survive in the jungle and are unable to purposively carve their own way in the world. They are often dependent on employers, clients and marketing departments and have difficulty creating a clearing in this jungle. Designers in other branches find themselves in the same situation. In my work as a cultural capital producer, in which I am concerned with improving the culture of business, I am increasingly confronted with this situation. For this reason I decided to start up a project. Together with the Berlin philosopher Hajo Eickhoff, I have been working for one year on a tool that has the potential to bridge the gap between designers and clients, for example. The project eventually resulted in a series of norms for designers under the title *Form: Ethik.*

Form: Ethik is a manual, a navigation tool and a source of inspiration for those whose designs and the practical applications of their wisdom have an influence on society . The book has received more than twenty awards and the first edition was sold out instantly. In the meantime the second edition is almost no longer available. Every day Hajo Eickhoff and I receive requests to make the ethics alphabet, which is included in the book, available via email since it provides designers with inspiration and orientation. In the hope that it will help the reader in a professional, cultural, private and social respect, we are publishing it below.

ETHICS ALPHABET

ALERTNESS
When you are alert you perceive your surroundings, fellow men and yourself as a single whole. The part is also a whole and determines the quality of the product's form.

BALANCE
Design is concerned with an interplay of changes that we call balance. This balance has to be maintained. Those who are aware that our senses are the antennas with which we sound out imbalances in ourselves and our surroundings realise that balance represents something meaningful. By giving meaning to something we create a construction whereby balance is maintained. In the case of professional involvement this meaningfulness consists in usefulness for society. What is of prime importance here is not society as an economic entity, but society as culture. Changes influence this culture and the balance between nature and culture.

CHARAKTER/CHARACTER
Character stands for the ethical motivation to think, feel and act. This concept, of Greek origin, means die, stereotype or pattern, and stands for that which is imprinted, minted, for those character traits that together form the unique essence of a person, thing or company. It is there that creativity and thinking unfold, where the characters of an individual and an enterprise match each other. Companies with character create products with character, products that are of high quality, beautiful and durable. Such companies also have no difficulty in presenting themselves publicly as honest and sincere.

DENKEN/THINKING
Thinking is one of those activities that you can completely submerge yourself in to your heart's content. You can think, reflect or think along with, or on behalf of, others. With thinking the world is rediscovered every day anew. With reflecting you can help others. The word 'method' is derived from this. Thinking along is a condition for a functioning democracy, for a functioning community. It is not for nothing that thanking is similar to thinking. Thanking means remembering something.

ETHICS
The Kantian logic of the categorical imperative is surprisingly clear. It represents the key to ethical conduct: putting yourself in the other's place and making your own standards also apply to the other. Ethics thus becomes our communal

ship, traversing crises, passages and paradigms. Joseph Brodsky once said that aesthetics is the mother of ethics because the only people who cannot be manipulated are those who develop their own taste. This means that at a higher level, if you regard the mother figure as a higher level, ethics functions as a sign. Design is not only a creative process, but also an ethical one that is condensed into a sign that you can perceive with your senses and fathom how it remains in balance.

FREEDOM
A free spirit – a spirit that is under no pressure and has freedom of movement – is able to put itself in another's position. The free spirit is an open spirit. The realisation that we have responsibilities is particularly to be found among free spirits. Freedom is one of our sources of strength and vitality. Even if you acknowledge that some things are inevitable, which comes down to the recognition and acknowledgement of compulsion, the idea that you can freely decide is an alleviating and integrating force that refers to a higher aim.

GLÜCK/HAPPINESS
'Know yourself.' Self-knowledge and the pursuit of happiness are inextricably bound up with one another. Happiness means that the soul is in harmony with morality. A happy person has a dignified attitude and is able to give more than he needs to receive.

HALTUNG/ATTITUDE
The spiritual and spatial attitude of people and companies is expressed in the relation they maintain with their past. A good attitude comprises: protecting, waiting and contemplating. A good attitude is a cultural attitude with which designers express their capacities, their intentions and their goals. Owing to their inner attitude, clients and designers who work on the ethics of form are kindred spirits.

INSPIRATION
Whoever follows a star, pursues an idea, does this with his head held high, at the same time taking a deep breath. Seeing as the word 'inspiration' means blowing in, inspiration coincides with the idea that something can be brought to life or be animated by means of breath. Inspiration is the animated idea that incites deeds. Inspiration cannot be forced, but moves forward on the breath of life. That is to say, if we are connected with life and the world, if we let go of what we have consumed and open ourselves to the new.

*JUGENDLICHKEIT/*YOUTHFULNESS

To what extent can you retain your youthfulness when it comes to practice, in the interests of yourself and of your work for the community? Idealistic, fresh, fervent, inquisitive – young people are still fresh because the pleasure of the new has not yet been relativised by routine. Their idealism and eagerness to learn are nourished by the urgent necessity for an individual orientation. Youth also means designing a crisis, namely the crisis of becoming mature, which is tackled with fantasy and passion. One should design oneself in a way that everyone can relate to, since it is a process that takes place not in isolation but within society, and society is changed by it as well. The young generation always puts its finger on the weak spots of morality – free from all sobriety.

*KREATIVITÄT/*CREATIVITY

Culture can blossom thanks to creativity, since creativity is deviant. Creativity gives rise to a series of ideas with which a problem can be solved. It deviates from standard patterns of thought and develops ideas that sometimes go against the social mainstream. There is no place for intuition here. Creativity is a quest that from a biological point of view is crucial to survival.

LEARNING

Learning has consequences for conduct. If you regard your work, or designing, or life itself as a learning process, then you publicly acknowledge that you are open to changes that are necessary for your conduct, your life, your designs and life itself.

MOTIVATION

Designers stimulate motivation. Motivation stands for pleasure and passion, for stimuli and vitality. And for a heightened quality of life, since an appeal is made to all the senses. The thing is to create motivation, to strengthen the meaning of life and to lend dignity to people. In this way life acquires a particular direction – towards a responsible way of doing business.

THE NEW

Unlike nature, culture does not have powers at its disposal with which it can cure itself. Therefore one has to be frugal with nature and renew it from time to time. Nature in all its various manifestations should always serve as the starting point for designing, since nature is the norm and the inexhaustible source that stimulates newness.

ORIGINALITY

Originality relates to origins. The value of originality stems from the order of the beginning and the order of the unique. The origin gives rise to energies. That is why reviewing one's own origin, one's own source, is tantamount to refreshment.

PROFESSIONALITY
Professionality brings rationality and passion into balance. Passion is a remedy for the decline of creativity, while rationality creates the conditions for craftsmanship and the consistent elaboration of an idea. Professionality and profession mean giving evidence and having a calling – dedication and engagement.

QUALITY
Quality should be main thing of concern for every designer. Everything that exists in the world has an essence. The hallmarks of essence are its nature, value and uniqueness. The essence is the 'what' of something – its *quale*, or quality. Nature has value in itself, it is precious and represents the standard for quality. This is what designers should orient themselves towards when designing products. Quality is a duty. It has a salutary effect and endows life with content, so that people become motivated. A good form, a practical and surprising function and reliable material appeal to people since the receptive capabilities of the senses are thereby enhanced, diversity is maintained and people are enabled to perceive nuances and gradations. Quality makes people light. They are lifted up and their creative forces stimulated.

RUHE/QUIET
Whoever seeks peace and quiet has to be able to free himself from everyday obligations. Finding peace and quiet, looking into yourself, knowing your own strength, but also perceiving weaknesses. Recognising that results have causes, and that these causes always lead to the same results. That is why it is good to incorporate peace into the work and not to be in a hurry – to slow down – so as to prevent the design from being short-winded. Designs can then last a long time, so that they are not subjected to rapidly changing fashions and trends.

SCHÖNHEIT/BEAUTY
Beauty means a pause in the world. Whoever keeps body, spirit and soul in harmony can create beauty. Whoever takes care of the soul – the non-organic organ – maintains contact with the higher, since the soul connects beauty with love and allows man to create something that is greater than himself.

TUGEND/PURITY
Whoever trains himself to listen well is alert to the arguments of others, is tolerant, has the courage to be himself and does not flinch from serving others; such a person maximalises the strength, clarity and purity of his ideas and deeds.

UNIVERSE

The world forms a unity and the totality of being is the universe. Like the parts of a design, each part of it transcends itself and refers to the whole. The design of the world is hidden. It can be surmised, however, in the stars, in nature and in objects of great beauty that have been made by the hands of man. Ethics is a general and universal notion that man has to acknowledge and apply to the entire global community. For designers it can be important that they remain open for the invisible design of the universe, since in this way they can feel responsible for their fellow men, their environment and future generations.

VERANTWORTUNG/RESPONSIBILITY

Whoever recognises the connection between nature, culture and products is capable of developing a view of mankind from the Creation to the future and back again to the present, since this connection demonstrates the unity of ideas, words, deeds and things, and gives sense to life. One should also take responsibility for what one neglects to do. That's how great people act.

WERTE/VALUES

Why do I do what I do? Am I doing it for myself or does it also have a general use? People's destiny is determined by who they meet, what they choose, by who or what they are themselves chosen, where they are active or where they draw back. This is why personal systems of values and forms must be developed for contemporary designing, since these help in finding or confirming one's own way. Art and design do not come into being according to democratic agreements.

XENOPHILIA

It is essential to be open to strangers and to the foreign if the earth's cultures want to come closer to one another on the path to a global community. Xenophilia is love for others and for the foreign. The foreign can serve as a starting point for developing yourself and for expanding your language of forms, given that every culture has its own forms and realities.

YIN AND YANG

This ancient Chinese division entails the unity of opposites. A circular area consisting of two elements that form a unity, each one symbolising a basic principle: material and spiritual, or female and male. Designers may not limit themselves to an aesthetic solution of a problem, but should work within the scope of unity and opposites: of economy and ecology, of technology and culture, of past and future, of ethics and aesthetics.

ZUKUNFT/FUTURE

Designing the future is a way to be alert. The future cannot be predicted, but it can be thought about and designed. Designers should devise a vision of the future within the framework of a world-encompassing ethics. People should be in a position to also live a decent and peaceful life in the future, as well as in a world with rapid technological developments and more and more interventions in nature. What is needed for this is a form of conduct that stems directly from a vision of the future: the wish and the commitment to create as much space as possible in the present for the future of life on planet Earth.

The symbol of balance.

WILLIAM MCDONOUGH / MICHAEL BRAUNGART

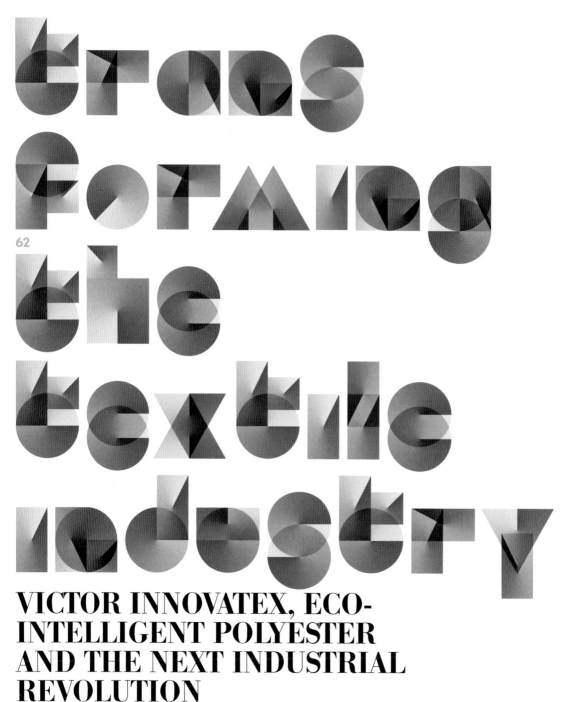

transforming the textile industry

VICTOR INNOVATEX, ECO-INTELLIGENT POLYESTER AND THE NEXT INDUSTRIAL REVOLUTION

The North American textile industry is taking a beating. In 2001 alone, nearly 67,000 textile workers in the United States lost their jobs. Industry giants such as Burlington and Guilford Mills filed for bankruptcy, while more than 100 US and Canadian plants shut down. As the value of Asian currency continued its freefall, US textile exports dropped for the sixth straight year and industry leaders pleaded with Congress to help slow the wave of cheap apparel flooding the market.

Worldwide, textile producers face other challenges. The industry that launched the Industrial Revolution has long illustrated some of its most notorious design failures. About one half of the world's wastewater problems are linked to the production of textile goods, and many of the chemicals used to dye and finish fabrics are known to harm human health. Often, the clippings from carpet or fabric mills are so loaded with dangerous chemicals they are handled like toxic waste, while the products made from these materials are considered safe for use in the home.

The crisis in the textile industry reverberates widely. More than 32 million people worldwide work in clothing manufacturing plants. Millions more work in mills producing the fabrics that surround us, such as seating, drapes, and carpeting. In short, the industry's material flows affect nearly everyone: From the vast appetite of its supply chain – including one third of the production of the chemical industry – to a distribution network that spans the world, textiles are quite literally woven into the fabric of life. It is an industry crucial to the human prospect and in dire need of innovation.

This is not news to Alain Duval, president of Victor Innovatex, a family-owned and run contract fabric producer headquartered in Saint-Georges, Quebec. Duval has been working in the textile industry since he was a boy, when he sorted wool for recycling in his grandfather's mill. Upon assuming leadership of the company from his father in the early 1980s, Duval saw that Victor would not survive if it continued to produce woolen goods for the commodities market – a market in which it would always be undersold by manufacturers in countries with a steady supply of low cost labor. Instead, Duval focused the company on manufacturing high-quality fabrics for the contract furniture market. Melding Victor's heritage as a lean manufacturer to an increasingly strong interest in new technologies and environmental responsibility, Duval staked the company's future on an ethic of innovation within a well-defined market niche.

His bet paid off. Victor has not only survived the economic crisis in the textile industry, it has flourished, continuing to prosper while becoming a recognized industry leader in ecologically sound design. In 2001, Victor introduced Eco-Intelligent™ Polyester, the first polyester produced and dyed with all environmentally safe ingredients, including a new catalyst that replaces the metalloid antimony, a known toxicant. Developed in partnership with MBDC and its German sister company EPEA, Eco-Intelligent Polyester is designed to be safely recycled into new fabric at the end of its life, with none of the hazardous by-products of traditional polyester recycling. It is a truly revolutionary fabric – a healthy alternative for the textile trade and a signal of hope for human industry.

POLYESTER AND THE FUTURE OF RECYCLING

This breakthrough in polymer design could have an enormous impact on the textile industry. Polyester is a key synthetic fiber. Its high performance and durability make it the world's most popular polymer. Roughly 11 million tons of polyester are produced each year, one half of the total annual production of all synthetic fibers. Polyester is also recyclable. In fact, polyester recycling is so common, and so widely perceived as environmentally sound, it is now *de rigueur* for fabric manufacturers to carry a recycled polyester product. Industry also uses reclaimed polyester for fuel, as do the poor in many Third World countries.

Unfortunately, traditionally produced and recycled polyester is far from optimal. Most polyester is manufactured using antimony as a catalyst. Antimony is toxic to the heart, lungs, liver and skin. Antimony trioxide, a by-product of polymer production, can cause chronic bronchitis and emphysema upon long-term inhalation. Antimony trioxide leaches from polyester fibers during the high-temperature dye process and appears in the wastewater. Recycling polyester, another high-temperature process, creates the same wastewater problems; burning it releases antimony trioxide into the air. Indeed, the conventional manufacture of polyester is so riddled with harmful chemicals, a recycling strategy that does not redesign the whole process could not hope to do anything but recapitulate toxic events.

Current recycling practices for nearly all materials tend to be high-tech waste management strategies for low-quality products. Rather than regaining valuable materials for perpetual reuse in high quality goods, much recycling is actually downcycling, a reduction in the value of material over time. The recycling of plastics, for example, often mixes different polymers to produce a hybrid of lower quality, which is then used to produce something amorphous and cheap, such as speed bumps – a spiraling loss of value that ultimately ends in the landfill. And, as we have seen, recycling of this kind is often a toxic process.

Eco-Intelligent Polyester changes the story. By starting the design process at the molecular level, MBDC and EPEA were able to analyze every ingredient in polyester and choose dyestuffs, auxiliary chemicals, and a catalyst that are safe and environmentally sound. This creates the opportunity to transform recycling from a costly waste management strategy into a system that eliminates the concept of waste.

Here's how. When product design begins with the selection of healthful ingredients, materials such as Eco-Intelligent Polyester can be safely and perpetually used, reclaimed, and reused in high-quality products. In fact, closing the loop on material flows in this way only makes sense if the material is designed to be ecologically safe. Otherwise, the closed loop cycles become contaminated with toxic chemicals, triggering health concerns and a downward spiral in value. But when design begins at the molecular level, synthetic products can be conceived as technical nutrients, which are materials specifically designed to 'feed', or be returned to, industrial systems without any harmful effects. Materials made from natural ingredients can be designed as biological nutrients, which can be safely returned to the earth. From this perspective, industrial waste is no longer problematic. Instead, waste equals food. Products designed as food, or nutrients, for technical and biological systems are the future of effective recycling.

AN ENERGETIC INDUSTRY LEADER

Eco-Intelligent Polyester is the first textile designed as a technical nutrient. It's no surprise it emerged from Victor Innovatex. Victor is a small company with a tradition of quality manufacturing, sound environmental management, and strong, collaborative relationships with its customers. During the 1990s it incorporated new spinning and high speed weaving technologies, a responsive product development process, and customer service goals all targeted toward becoming a leaner, faster, more efficient company. These innovations, paired with Victor's energetic cultivation of the contract furniture market, led to extraordinary growth for the company.

Victor's goal, however, was 'not to grow big' but to work closely with its clients to 'do big things'. The opportunity to do a truly extraordinary thing came in 1999, when one of Victor's customers, Susan Lyons of DesignTex, approached the company about developing with MBDC and EPEA an ecologically intelligent synthetic textile, a technical nutrient. Here was an opportunity to further differentiate the company within its market niche while developing a stronger partnership with one of its key clients. It was also a chance, said Victor's Marketing Manager, Janelle Henderson, 'to do the next great thing'.

'We are very good at being lean', she said. 'We raised the bar on lean manufacturing. We raised the bar on quality and consistency. But the time had come to take the next step.'

For Henderson, and for Victor's leadership, developing an innovative polyester designed to maintain high value through many product life-cycles – a source of food for industrial systems – felt like a sensible leap. 'When you eliminate the concept of waste you eliminate all the problems associated with conventional industrial production', she said. 'For us, the idea that "waste equals food" just makes sense.'

So Victor took the next step, engaging MBDC and EPEA in the design of its new polyester. The firms began by identifying an environmentally sound catalyst to replace antimony. They had been seeking a new polymer catalyst since discovering during the design process of a new shower gel that antimony was leaching from the gel's plastic packaging into the product itself. By the time their work with Victor began, they knew of effective alternatives and specified for Eco-Intelligent Polyester a titanium- and silica-based catalyst with no toxic effects.

Next, MBDC and EPEA analyzed all the dyes and auxiliaries Victor used in the manufacture of polyester, trimming a list of 57 chemicals to fifteen. Of those, several were replaced with more environmentally sound chemicals, polishing off a new, totally safe palette. The chemical assessment and material evaluation guidelines of the MBDC Protocol are now being used by Victor's designers and engineers and have become part of an ongoing design process geared to producing fabrics with wholly positive impacts on human and environmental health.

FROM PERFORMANCE TO PARTNERSHIPS

We sometimes call Eco-Intelligent Polyester 'the polyester environmentalists can love'. But it's also a polyester Victor's designers, engineers, sales people and executives can appreciate. Along with being optimized for environmental safety, Eco-Intelligent Polyester offers all the performance benefits of conventional polyester. There are no limitations on color choice and it can be woven in any jacquard pattern in a great variety of styles.

While designers love the aesthetic values, Victor's executives think Eco-Intelligent Polyester simply makes good business sense. Developing the new fabric, said Alain Duval, 'was perfectly in line with our "lean thinking" philosophy, yet it was even more advanced'. The new protocol, he said, extended thoughtful consideration of materials throughout the design process, from sources in the supply chain to the impact on the earth of 'every aspect of the product and the manufacturing process'. As a result, Victor has been able to satisfy the needs of its customers – furniture manufacturers such as Steelcase, as well as textile distributors DesignTex, Carnegie and C.F. Stinson – for cutting edge solutions to environmental problems.

Eco-Intelligent Polyester might be of only passing interest if it were Victor's lone environmentally safe product. But the company's leadership has taken bold steps to fulfill the promise of their new fabric, launching a series of initiatives to integrate ecologically intelligent design at every level of the business. Engineers are applying the MBDC Protocol to product design; Victor's facilities are increasingly using energy from renewable sources; marketing efforts are built on communicating the benefits of products that go beyond waste reduction to benefit the environment at all phases of their life cycle; and strategic efforts throughout the company are building partnerships with other businesses that share Victor's vision.

Together, these efforts add up to a product development process Victor calls its Eco-Intelligence Initiatives (EII). As Sales and Marketing Director Jean François Gagnon said, product development is 'not just about the product'.

'Yes, Eco-Intelligent Polyester is a wonderful fabric', he said. 'But in designing and producing new fabrics we also want our manufacturing process to meet the highest environmental standards, we want to tap into the knowledge and passion of our designers and engineers, and we want to develop partnerships with like-minded companies. The environmental agenda has to be shared.'

Thus far the partnerships that support the expanding EIIproduct line have yielded Eco-Intelligent Polyester and Climatex® LifeguardFR TM, a fabric woven of organically grown, compostable fibers. While the new polyester is a technical nutrient, Climatex LifeguardFR, produced in collaboration with the Swiss textile mill, Rohner, is a biological nutrient designed to be safely returned to the earth after use. This pair of new fabrics makes Victor the first company ever to produce and market both a biological and technical nutrient, a landmark in ecologically intelligent design.

As Gagnon makes clear, Victor could not have achieved this pioneering role alone. Victor cannot sustain it alone either. By developing environmentally sound fabrics it has taken the first, crucial step toward safely closing the loop on the flow of industrial materials. Building a system for the reclamation of those materials is a challenge for the entire industry.

It's a challenge some are accepting. Textile makers, fabric distributors, and furniture manufacturers have already begun to come together to explore the design of a take-back program for textile recycling. Though some in the US textile industry dismiss the idea, we see hopeful precedents. The automotive industry, for example, has begun to appreciate the economic benefits of reusing valuable materials and is already moving toward implementing take-back programs. In Europe, the reclamation of automotive materials is the law. As other industries follow suit, companies such as Victor will be perfectly positioned to offer value-added materials designed for safe reclamation and re-use. A further step could include making polyester from renewable resources, transforming it into a fully biodegradable material that flows in biological cycles.

What we're talking about here is nothing less than the Next Industrial Revolution. Can textile manufacturers, with their enormous influence on the world economy, recover from their current woes to lead this transformation of human industry? We think Victor Innovatex is showing how they might. Clearly, North American apparel makers are in for an uphill battle as they compete with inexpensive imports in the commodities market. But if restructuring is the order of the day, why not reshape the textile industry following the lead of successful companies, such as Victor and Rohner, that are creating economic value with innovation, intelligence and good design? Wouldn't it be fitting and delightful if the constructive, 25-year discussion of environmental issues birthed by Rachel Carson's Silent Spring were directed by business leaders toward product quality? Imagine the textile industry renewed by the insights of ecology. Imagine industrialized nations projecting their strength through the export of life-affirming products that bring economic, social, and ecological value to the entire world. Instead of a legacy of toxic materials, low wages and ecological destruction, let's build on today's innovations and create a legacy of nutritious materials, prosperity and health for all species.

MANUFACTURE

TECHNICAL METABOLISM
PRODUCTS OF SERVICE

ECOLOGY

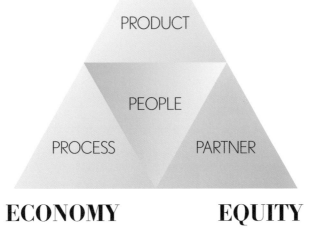

PRODUCT

PEOPLE

PROCESS   PARTNER

ECONOMY   EQUITY

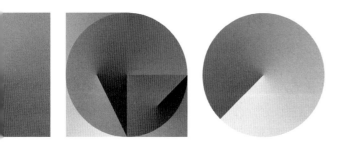

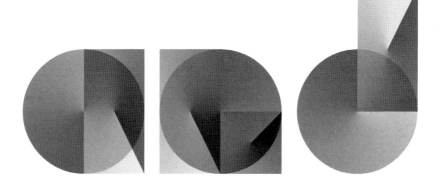

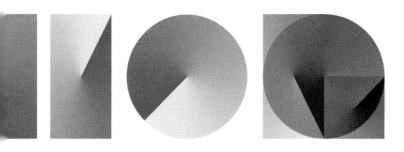

What does the wardrobe of the future look like? A printer able to print out clothes, shoes and accessories will in the future perhaps be supplied along with a wardrobe cupboard. A seed box for self-growing textiles is also one of the possibilities. And in the corner of the cupboard there will probably be a charger for powering LED patterns in elegant evening wear. The amount of basic clothing items will be minimal, since the shirts of the future will not get dirty, will not stink and will never wear out – thanks to active particles coupled to textile fibres with the aid of nanotechnology. What is certain is that future developments will be aimed at sustainability, so there will be an increased demand for biodegradable and environment-friendly materials. In the future environmental laws will impose more and more restrictions regarding overproduction and waste disposal. All these developments will cause major changes in production chains. Five experts involved on a daily basis with the application or development of new materials set out their ideas for the future.

Technological materials are mainly finding their way to the consumer via high-tech sportswear. Yet most of the technological developments that are actually being applied in fashion remain at the level of gadgets. An example of this is the Hug Shirt, a shirt that responds to SMS messages from a sweetheart with vibrations and warmth. Or shirts with a screen on which you can make your own texts or on which images appear. Clothing that changes colour with an increase in heart rate or body temperature is very special in terms of technology, but who would want to be such an 'open book' for their surroundings?

SCIENTISTS AND DESIGNERS

There is a huge gulf between the world of (fashion) designers and that of scientists, which often makes collaboration difficult. The difference in how new developments are approached is given as the reason for this. A designer is mainly interested in the application of a new material and a scientist in its properties. Yet different disciplines can stimulate each other and together can create fantastic projects. More and more attention is being devoted to collaboration in further education and academies, since there is a realisation that the only basis now for innovation in fashion lies with technology – everything else has already been thought of. But that was the conclusion that Paco Rabanne had already come to in 1966: 'I defy anyone to design a hat, coat or dress that hasn't been done before... The only new frontier left in fashion is the discovery of new materials.'
There are fascinating examples of collaborations between fashion designers and scientists. One important designer in this respect is Hussein Chalayan, who often makes use of the knowledge of experts from other disciplines. He is known for his LED Dress and his Mechanical Dress, for which he worked with the

German electrical engineer Moritz Waldemeyer. For his first solo show in 1997 Martin Margiela worked together with a Dutch microbiologist who helped him create various colours and textures by using yeast and bacteria. The young New York designer Angel Chang makes wearable garments using 'intelligent' fabrics that change colour. For each garment she calls in the help of a technology expert.

MIRACLE MATERIALS

One development that is already playing an important role in textiles, and will become even more important in the future, is nanotechnology. The idea says something about the scale at which a particular technology is applied. Nanotechnology works at the unimaginable level of a billionth of a metre. By way of comparison, microtechnology, of microfibre cloths and microcapsules in cosmetics fame, works at the level of a millionth of a metre. Nanotechnology is used within various fields of science, including biotechnology, medicine and chemistry. It is expected that the market for textiles produced with nanotechnology will grow from 13.7 billion euros in 2007 to 115 billion in 2012.[1] With nanotechnology it is possible to endow natural materials such as cotton with the properties of synthetic materials by linking 'foreign' molecules to the cotton molecules. The most well-known examples of nanotechnology in textiles are the self-cleaning, bacteria-resistent and water-repellent materials that are frequently used in sportswear and uniforms.

LAYER BY LAYER

A second important technique is 3D Printing, otherwise known as rapid manufacturing, rapid prototyping and layering manufacturing. 3D Printing involves building up a three-dimensional object by spraying layers of a rapidly hardening, liquid material on top of each other. Another method of 3D Printing is to use lasers to fuse together particles in a powder bed layer by layer according to a particular pattern. A 3D machine is directly controlled by a CAD/CAM design on the computer. The technique was invented in the 1980s for making single or small series of prototypes, but in recent years it has been rapidly adopted by the design world. The first step towards three-dimensional printing of textiles was taken in 1999 by the Dutch company Freedom of Creation.

---

[1]   Source: Ministry of Economic Affairs, the Netherlands.

'FASHION DESIGNERS OFTEN DON'T REALISE THAT THERE'S ANOTHER WORLD OUT THERE, WHERE NOT EVERYONE WEARS LANVIN OR WALKS AROUND ON TOWERING STILETTO HEELS.'

The New York fashion designer Angel Chang combines functional clothing and technology into high fashion. Her first collection, for spring 2007, was noticed straight away by *The New York Times*, *Newsweek*, Style.com and *Elle*. Angel received a number of fashion prizes, including the Ecco Domani Fashion Foundation Award 2007. For autumn 2008 she devised a cardigan that automatically gets warmer as the body temperature decreases, and for spring this year a light red dress that shows the map of Manhattan when the temperature changes. For carrying out her ideas Angel often works together with scientists and manufacturers of industrial products, a collaboration that requires clear agreements and in particular a lot of persuasiveness. Her ultimate aim is to design the ideal wardrobe for the modern, busy woman.

What are you working on at the moment?

'Right now I'm working on the spring 2009 collection. We're in the phase of research and concept development. In addition I'm having discussions with companies about possible collaborations so that I can design more than the current two collections that I present each year, and to look together for ways to improve the fashion industry as a whole.'

Which technologies did you use in your latest collections?

'My most recent collection for autumn 2008 is about travel and future fashion. The idea was to develop a wardrobe that would drastically reduce the amount of luggage. Some garments can be changed from tops to dresses, others have removable scarves and can be worn upside down for example. In collaboration with a German artist, Johannes Wohnseifer, I've been using heat-sensitive ink. He sent me a design for a map of the world divided into different time zones. When it's nighttime in Germany then that part of the print is in a dark colour, while the other side of the garment, which stands for New York, changes to 'daylight' yellow when you touch it. The collection also includes crease-resistant fabrics and a comfortable self-warming cashmere cardigan that works with a little rechargeable battery and heat-conducting silver filaments.'

How did you get the idea of combining technology with fashion?

'When I was working at Donna Karan as Design Assistant a large part of my work consisted of looking for vintage clothes, so as to inspire the designers. It struck me that we were mainly modernising old styles from the past and that none of the designs contributed to our modern way of life. On the Internet I found all sorts of interesting discoveries by science students, from the mit Media Lab for example, where they were combining electronics with clothing. Their approach to clothing and wearables (wearable electronics) was exciting but they clearly needed some assistance in the field of fashion. At that time I was interested in making high-quality prototypes and showing fashion companies all the things that were possible with technology and textiles. But when I showed my ideas to the design team at Donna Karan, nobody understood how this could be translated into clothing. So this inspired me to bring out my own collection in which I could combine fashion and technology.'

Do you use technology to distinguish yourself from the rest of the fashion world?

'I see technology mainly as a means to give women more freedom in wearing clothes. A design like a cardigan that warms up by itself and adapts itself to your body temperature means that we don't have to keep changing clothes or putting on more layers. The collection gives women a choice of clothing to match

76

a busy life. Women like to wear beautiful clothes and of course it's even better if these are crease-resistant or waterproof.'

What technical problems have you encountered in your work?

'There are so many. We once developed an accessory set with flashing led lights that reacted to one another when they were no more than ten metres apart. But the circuit board was too big for the accessory. For a smaller version we had to go to a special factory that only wanted to work with a large minimum order. There is no formula for the things we do – we learn through trial and error. None of my factories wants to work with my heat-sensitive ink, for example. So we have to ship the ink from Japan and then look for someone here who is prepared to take a risk with a 'strange' product. Through my work I often have to motivate people who work in traditional ways and convince them that it's good to overstep one's bounds now and then and to try out new things. No other fashion designer is doing what we're doing. So we're the first ones to run into these problems, but we're also the first to reap the benefits when it all goes well.'

You're amazed at the gap that exists between scientists and designers. What do you notice yourself regarding this?

'It's difficult to maintain a high level of quality when you're working with people who aren't feeling materials like silk, chiffon or cashmere every day. So the biggest challenge for me is to make clear to a non-fashion public what I mean. Fashion designers often don't realise that there's another world out there, where not everyone wears Lanvin or walks around on towering stiletto heels.'

How do think this collaboration can improve?

'A good place to improve collaboration in the fashion industry is the production company. It is here that new materials are developed, and design and development coincide. As far as education is concerned, I think it would be good if students from different disciplines were taught in the same building. This would make it easier to stimulate multidisciplinary projects.'

Has there been an evolution in the technical materials that you are using?

'Yes, the way we're using materials has become more complex. In the beginning we were using the heat-sensitive ink straight from the pot. And there are only a few colours available. Now we've found a way to mix the colours and so we can make an infinite series of colours that react to different temperatures.'

What is your dream for the future?

'I'd like my company to become a meeting place, a sort of r&d centre where people can work together on new ideas and thus be able to influence the future of fashion. When I was working for other labels I had such a hectic schedule that I barely had time in the mornings to get dressed, let alone combine the right colours with each other. In the end I just wore black, since that was nice and easy, but it also made me depressed. My goal is to make a wardrobe for the future that will make women's lives easier and ensure that they have enough time left for the things they find important.'

What is your business plan for the next five years?

'To go on with what I'm doing now: build up a strong company around my label and focus more on designing travel clothing, since it's there that I see technology and fashion coming together. And I'll be advising chemical companies and electronics producers on how to launch their electronic and new materials in the fashion world.'

Simone de waart

'IF YOU WANT TO REMAIN INNOVATIVE AND TO MAKE A MARK, THEN YOU WILL HAVE TO COLLABORATE.'

Simone de Waart is a materials expert. After her studies at the Design Academy in Eindhoven, she started developing materials. Under the name Material Sense, she organises (international) exhibitions and workshops and publishes books about materials. In addition she is co-founder of the design studio Loods 5, tutor in 'materials in design' at the TU in Eindhoven and guest lecturer at other schools and art academies.

What is the aim of Material Sense?
'I started Material Sense five years ago with the aim of stimulating the development of new materials and ways to utilise them. We try to inspire creativity by discovering and investigating materials. With Material Sense I work together with universities. One of the public-oriented things we are doing is to make new materials known through a traveling exhibition. Each year I choose a different, topical theme and then bring together all the companies, designers and researchers who represent that theme in a good way. In the meantime Material Sense is traveling all over the world. And we've started producing books about materials. I also organise workshops under the name Material Tables®. Everything is aimed at linking designers, researchers and industry.'

Can you mention some of these new materials?
'One excellent product, I think, is fabric produced from stinging nettles. It has the potential to be a replacement for cotton and biological cotton, and the same goes for bamboo textile. My expectation is that more products will be developed, as these are fine materials and there will be a demand for new applications. What I also like is the recycling of pet bottles into textiles. The material looks good and it is easy to use. The colours are not so suitable for our market, but the patterns are great. This is more a material for interior fabrics or for bags; it's now being used a lot as a fabric for car interiors.'

Besides 'new' natural materials and synthetic replacements, there is a group of materials that acquire a different quality through the use of nanotechnology and biotechnology. Can you say something about these?

'What you're seeing now is a lot of work being done with coatings on materials. These coatings are often visible, so that it then acquires a synthetic finish, or it might become very tactile, feeling like the skin of fish for example. A lot is being done at this moment with ink that changes colour by reacting to heat or ultra-violet light. And we are continuing to imitate nature. For an exhibition in 2004 we presented all sorts of materials that have what is known as a lotus effect – these are materials that are self-cleansing. This effect is one of the first examples of biomimicry, an umbrella term for everything which is imitated from nature. As regards biotechnology, there's a lot being done with making materials grow like in nature. They're also involved with this at the tu. Seeing tissue grow in a petri dish is just crazy. As soon as you do that as a designer you inevitably end up in a very complicated ethical dilemma.'

How important is collaborating with other disciplines in your field?

'I think collaboration is very important and I believe that's where the future lies. If you want to remain innovative and to make a mark then you will have to collaborate, so that different expertises can complement each other. And that's easier said than done. When I started six years ago I did notice that collaboration did not always go so well, but in the meantime more and more companies are realising that innovative ideas arise through collaboration between different disciplines.'

Both designers and scientists are constantly on the lookout for new developments. Isn't that in itself a good starting point for collaboration?

'According to some experts, art and science have a common origin. But designers are focused on setting change in motion and scientists are focused on analysing and describing this change. We recently gave a workshop and one of the participating scientists described this process: "As a person you only have a limited amount of energy and you have to use this in a focused way in order to attain the best result. As a pure scientist I want to completely concentrate on science. Subsequently you need intermediaries who can be the link between other disciplines and can make the translation to application." This is the role we fulfil at Material Sense – that of network connector.'

What was done at the TU in Eindhoven in terms of collaboration between different disciplines?

'Before I started Material Sense I set up a collaboration between TU Eindhoven and the Design Academy in Eindhoven and supervised it for four years. If you want to achieve something with materials then you need to have examples that you can grasp. This was the reason why, together with and for the students, we set up a materials library. That was the start of the Material Sense Library. It was also a way of getting students to come together. Students are open for collaborating, but it works best with short, intensive projects in which you immediately get cracking together.'

Can you mention an example of a successful material created as a result of collaboration between scientists and designers?
'One excellent example, I think, is the material d3o. It was developed by English scientists with the aid of nanotechnology. Originally a byproduct of a research and development project, it is a soft, malleable material that, when subjected to abrupt force, changes into a hard, protective shell and then becomes soft again immediately afterwards. It's a fantastic material and to make sure that it is applied the scientists have set up a test lab, done extensive research and then started approaching major brands. d3o is now used as a component in protective clothing like ski suits, motorcycle suits, hats and gloves.'

Where do you see the biggest development taking place within the next ten years?
'In the integration of technology in materials and in the availability of sustainable materials. The collaboration between industries will deepen. You learn a technique in one industry and you then apply it in another. Materials like pvcthat are non-degradable and are a danger to the environment will disappear. And we will see a revaluation of old techniques and traditional customs, like the use of stinging nettles and fish skin in fashion. The addition of emotion to material is also something that we'll be seeing more and more. In the case of electronics integrated into textile, for example, emotions are increasingly being evoked by means of light, sound and motion change.'

84

Janne Kyttänen

'OUR GOAL IS TO REPLACE TRADITIONAL KNITTING.'

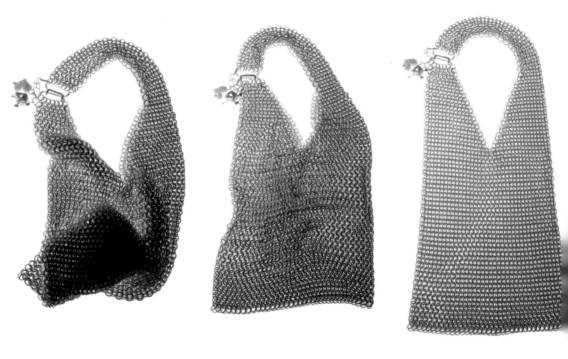

Nine years ago, the designers Janne Kyttänen (from Finland) and Jiri Even-huis (from the Netherlands) developed a process enabling textiles to be 'printed out' by using 'rapid prototyping' (also known as 3D Printing), which is used for making prototypes. The technique involves the building up of three-dimensional designs layer by layer. In 2006 Janne and Jiri founded the company Freedom of Creation, a design office specialising in developing products and concepts for 3D Printing. The applications of this technology in the fashion world are revolutionary and in the (distant) future can have major consequences for traditional production chains. Janne Kyttänen explains what the possibilities are of 3D Printing.

What is the advantage of 3D Printing for your design work?

'It's the same as the relationship between a computer and a typewriter. It's the next step in creation. I was used to making a whole lot of sketches, so for me it's a dream come true, since I no longer have to go to the workshop to fuse and stick parts together. It's fantastic, you make a design and a few days later a man comes knocking at your door with the finished product.'

What are the limitations of 3D Printing?

'At the moment there are still a lot of limitations. We need to have more variety in materials, such as flexible, lasting and strong materials. The costs of 3D Printing are quite high. And the speed is also a limitation. Injection moulding is much quicker. But ultimately, if you were to have such a machine at home, then it's faster than the whole process of going to a shop to purchase a product.'

What is one of the first things that could happen with 3D Printing?

'It's already happening. Our designs are very complex, it's almost impossible for someone to copy them. But once someone is in possession of the file he can do whatever he wants with it. We're busy setting up a worldwide production network and we've got production companies all over the world. If someone from Japan, for example, places an order, then we also produce it in Japan. Our goal is to expand this network, but at the same time the risk I just mentioned also increases.'

Why don't more suppliers concentrate on developing materials for the fashion business?

'It has to do with the size of the market. The car industry has been the driving force behind all the developments of rapid manufacturing. A lot of materials are initially developed for the car industry and for the medical world. Of course, I hope that will change. Special materials for lighting are now being made for the first time. This is because we've already been working on this for a number of years and now the industry sees it as a lively market.'

Do you work together with fashion labels?

'A few years ago, when we had developed the first textiles, we went to companies like Vuitton and Céline and told them we could make products for them that simply come out of a printer. Of course they were very interested, but they said, "Yes, guys, very impressive, but we've no idea what we can do with it. Go away." It was also a matter of communication. We were too early. Their reaction was: "Are you coming to tell us how we should do our work? We've been doing it this way for centuries." It takes time for companies to adapt their production chains and logistical and labour processes. That's the stumbling block, the technology is already there.'

You say that the technology is there, but does that mean you can actually make garments with 3D Printing?

'In principle it is possible to use wool and cotton for 3D Printing. Our goal is to replace traditional knitting, and that's why it is a revolutionary change. It's a question of material – everything that you can stack together is suitable for 3D Printing. We can already make stretch materials. We've made a dress from nylon and we can already make finer materials as well, in gold or silver. You can also think of shoe heels with special details that were previously impossible to produce. The problem is that the current machines are not large enough. But if someone can show that there's a potential billion dollar market for these textiles, then it won't be long before bigger machines are made.'

3D Printing at home – is that a realistic development?

'Yes, I think it's a question of time. I can't say when that will be possible, but it sounds logical to me. If your washing machine breaks down, then you have to look for a shop where you can order the part. Imagine that in such a case you simply go to "supplier.com/washing machines/broken part", where you can download the part and then print it out. But I don't believe that people will start making things themselves; designers will always be necessary.'

What would you like to make sometime with this technique?

'That's difficult to say. Every day is a great day for me since every day I can make something new. But sometime I would like to make something on a very small scale, or indeed on a very large scale. A few organisations are concerned with printing constructions. They can now print out a construction of five by five metres, they are printing concrete. So instead of spending months building a house, they claim they can do it in one day.'

**Ferd·
Visse**

VUILWEREND & VLOEISTOFBESTENDIG
ZEER EENVOUDIG TE REINIGEN

NANO-CLEAN®

ANTIBACTERIELE EIGENSCHAPPEEN
STOPT ACTIEF DE GROEI VAN BACTERIEN ZOALS BIJV. MRSA (99.9% BINNEN 2-4 UUR)

NANO-SILBER®

ANTI-M.R.S.A.

MEMBRANE COMFORT®
BUITENGEWOON ADEMEND EN WATERDICHT

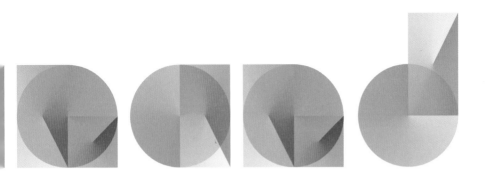

'I'M NOT A CHEMIST OR
TEXTILE DESIGNER, BUT
I DO LIKE TO DEVELOP
NEW THINGS.'

The Dutch firm Microcare specialises in inventing commercial, technological fabrics. In the nineties, Ferdinand Visser, Microcare's director, developed a special furnishing fabric using membrane film technology. This led to the use of nanotechnology in developing the fabric known as Microcare. The company's fabrics are produced in a cocktail bath.

What does the firm Microcare do?

'For Microcare I think up concepts for creating particular fabrics and then I go to manufacturers to have the products made. Our Microcare material is supplied with three high-tech additions. The first addition is Nano-Clean, an anti-stain and liquid repellent treatment. Then there's the addition of Nano-Silver, an antibacterial application used a lot in the medical world. The material is finished off with a membrane film that has good airflow and waterproof properties. As a firm you have to ask yourself what you want to concentrate on. The one technology replaces the other. In 2006, when we had mastered nanotechnology, we no longer needed bacteria-repellent capsules. I opt for nanotechnology, but someone else will opt for plasma technology. If nanotechnology turns out to be unsafe, then I have a problem.'

How did you end up in the world of nanotechnology?

'I started selling fabrics, mainly to the furniture industry, when I was twenty-four. Via furniture for the health service I got the idea in the late eighties to apply membrane film technology to microfibre fabrics. That was my first version of Microcare. From 1994 onwards I started developing it further. I'm not a chemist or textile designer, but I do like to develop new things.'

How do you add nano materials to fabrics?

'We've been involved with this development since 2004 and the biggest problem was to distribute the invisible particles across the fabric evenly and well. We solved it with a sort of cocktail consisting of particle of silver at nano level combined with a liquid. The fabric to be treated goes into a bath containing the nano cocktail. In the bath, to which dyes can also be added, there is a roller that impregnates the particles onto the molecules of the fibre. This is done at a certain temperature so that the particles continue to adhere. What you are actually doing is wrapping the bacteria with silver ions so that they no longer have a culture medium and are therefore unable to multiply.'

What are the disadvantages of nanotechnology?

'Nanotechnology is surrounded with an aura of mystery. Because you can't see nano particles it remains a notion that is difficult to grasp and has long been unfamiliar to the wider public. It also took several years before microfibres came on the market. In the meantime everyone knows about microfibre cloths, they've become accepted. After the introduction of our Microcare fabric with its nano application, copycats came on the market of course. The problem with nanotechnology is that it's not easy to control whether the technique is being used.'

Is there anything known yet about the possible dangers of nano-technology?

'It's a tricky subject. In the United States and Canada research is being done at the moment into what the harmful consequences of nanotechnology could be. Then you get the same discussion as you had with Teflon and Scotchgard. Is it harmful if particles of the materials come in or on the body? If you rub a fabric to which "foreign" nanoparticles have been added, do these particles indeed continue to adhere? The fact is that nanoparticles that have been "stuck" to fabric by means of temperature adhere better than microparticles.'

With nanotechnology you can in theory add all sorts of 'new' characteristics to existing materials. How do you see developments in the future?

'Wool will be enriched with applications of nanotechnology, but new natural fabrics are already in production, such as fabrics made of maize fibre and of course stinging nettles. Cotton is interesting to replace because of all the chemicals that are needed in the cultivation and processing. I expect there to be a turn from synthetic materials to enriched natural materials. The next step for me is to endow natural materials with the properties of synthetic fibres. But there is much more to think about as regards structure and material. Like the three-dimensional 'spacer fabrics', which are hybrid fabrics made of different synthetic and natural fibres. These can then be combined with nano applications. I think that's what we'll be seeing in the future. The crazier it is, the more chance that there's a fantastic future product in it. Safety is a weakness, but work is being done on the certification of nanotechnology.'

'STUDENTS ARE REALISING THAT A DESIGNER HAS TO BE ABLE TO DO MORE THAN JUST DESIGN.'

The course in Fashion Technology at the Hogeschool Gent devotes a lot of attention to the combination of technology and design. In 2006 the Hogeschool Gent initiated the setting up of Motiv, the innovation platform for fashion technology in Flanders. One of the aims of the platform is to support industry in switching from traditional to technologically advanced products. Alexandra de Raeve teaches at the Hogeschool Gent and coordinates the programme in Fashion Technology. In addition she investigates and develops new materials. Collaboration between different disciplines is very important and begins with the students.

What is the Hogeschool Gent's speciality as regards fashion and textile technology?

'The Hogeschool Gent offers unique programmes in fashion technology and textile technology within the departments of Technology and Applied Engineering Sciences. The Academy department also offers programmes in fashion design and textile design – these are purely artistic courses. The programme in fashion technology offers a mix of creativity, marketing and above all technology. The expertise of the programme in fashion technology lies in the application of new materials and assemblage techniques, CAD and the development of new products.'

What are the latest developments concerning materials at the Hogeschool Gent?

'One of the things we are involved in is devising new printing methods for fabrics. By applying a special coating to fabrics we are succeeding in strongly increasing the intensity and vividness of pigment prints. And in collaboration with a Flemish company we have developed an anti-friction material under the name ReSkin, which can be applied in such sports as cycling, rowing and horse racing, as well as in the medical world.'

Do you see a shift taking place from fashion students and scientists to a combination of the two?

'Students are realising that a designer must be able to do more than just design. Students of Fashion Technology in Ghent are given the possibility to take an optional artistic course in the Academy department. In recent years the clothing and fashion sector in Europe has evolved into a knowledge-driven industry. Product development, product preparation, quality control and distribution are activities that continue to happen in Belgium, so companies are looking for broadly educated people who have knowledge not only of product design but also of the processes involved in producing the product economically and in an ecologically responsible way.'

What changes do you think are needed in the curricula of educational institutes so as to achieve better collaboration?

'The Fashion Technology programme is revolutionary because we are already offering this combination. Furthermore, we have a lot of contact with colleagues in the department of Textile Technology. In the final year we do a project together concerning product development and business management. And we have regular contact with other fashion schools within Europe where, with one or two exceptions, we time and time again come to the conclusion that our mix of design and technology is unique.'

Do you work with 3D printers at the Hogeschool Gent?

'Three-dimensional designing is dealt with in seminars. The technology is not yet fully applicable. I also doubt whether this will mean the end of making prototypes. Our students are also working with special printing techniques in order to achieve three-dimensional effects. One group of students, for example, has developed washing instructions in relief for people who are visually impaired.'

Why are there still so few technological materials on offer in fashion?

'The applications are available, but for one reason or another they are not employed by the fabric manufacturers. Because the costs are high the materials are often first used in the world of sports, as this is a branch where people are prepared to pay more for functional products. And with fashion the situation is different – functionality plays only a minor role. What I am seeing recently, though, is a consumer trend whereby, besides a beautiful design, people are starting to demand that clothing should be more functional.'

Do you think that new materials will replace cotton and wool?

'Perhaps in part, yes, but wool and cotton will always remain important. I find it hard to imagine that you would never replace an indestructible garment. Fashion simply changes. You can, however, think of interesting substitutes. Biopolymers, for example, are starting to be introduced more and more. There are different types. You have biopolymers that are made from maize or soya and are therefore extracted directly from the biomass. And then you have materials that are formed by chemical synthesis, like polylactic acids and compostable polyesters – a lot of research is being done into these. These materials have good properties – some are by nature bacteria resistant, which of course makes them very interesting for textiles. Using fabrics made from biopolymers means that you actually have a garment that is also biodegradable.'

And what do you see changing in the design process?

"The design process is very strongly computer driven. Patterns are currently being made with CAD/CAM, but the personalisation of clothing will also develop much further. Earlier you had the made-to-measure suit which was only available for the happy few, but now we're seeing it going towards a bespoke system that is accessible for all. You can indicate how you want your clothes to be. This trend will certainly become stronger.'

What would you like to develop yourself in terms of new materials?

'That's a difficult question. There is still so much to be done, certainly as regards fitting. And then there's still room for development in materials from which a lot has already been obtained, such as heat-regulating materials. A material that adapts itself to varying climactic conditions, but then really worked out in detail, and with a perfect fit, that's something I'd still like to develop.'

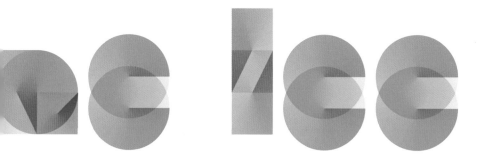

'A 100 % DURABLE MATE- RIAL IS THE 'HOLY GRAIL' AT THIS MOMENT.'

Suzanne Lee graduated from Central Saint Martins in London. After a career as a designer for various fashion labels she returned to Saint Martins as a researcher into materials. Her research brought her in contact with all sorts of new technologies and she decided to write a book about these: *Fashioning the Future*. This successful book features inspiring and sometimes bizarre examples of biotechnology, wearable electronics, self-growing materials and so-called 'intelligent' fabrics. Inspired by biotechnology, Suzanne has been developing a durable, self-growing material using bacteria, yeast and green tea. In 2006 she presented her first 'Bio Couture' garment: a denim jacket.

How did the idea of Bio Couture come about?
'It all started while I was doing research for the chapter on biotechnology in my book, *Fashioning the Future*, I interviewed an expert in materials, Dr David Hepworth, and we talked about how biology could help us in creating clothing. He told me it was possible to grow clothes. I found this to be an unimaginable idea. And that's where we started off from. I received some subsidy to make an initial prototype, which was the shirt I showed at *Fleshing Out*, the conference at V2 in Rotterdam and Amsterdam. Having demonstrated that we could make something from self-growing material, we were able to get another grant for a year-long project, which is now almost at an end.'

What are you involved in at the moment?

'I've just finished a motorcycle jacket decorated with studs, and I'm working on the process of painting a bomber jacket with fruit pulp. The next step in my project is to put together a team for the scientific part. We're going to have to do a lot of research so that we can control the material better. I'm looking for a team of microbiologists and we'll probably also need people to help with the production process, since I think there are several ways to obtain bacterial cellulose.'

What have been the most difficult parts of the project so far?

'We've not been able to solve one thing without creating a new series of problems. Developing a new material takes years. No sooner had we improved flexibility than another aspect got worse. What's more, the material becomes discoloured over time. After a period of six months the pieces change – they become hard or change colour. The pieces are unfortunately not as flexible as they were six months ago. So it's difficult to say which part is the hardest. The most difficult thing is the fact that we are developing a new fashion material. A material that is to be worn on the skin has to meet so many different demands compared with, say, an interior design fabric.'

Is it possible for someone from the fashion world to work with people from other disciplines?

'Fifteen years ago, when I first started looking for new technologies that could possibly be interesting for fashion, I went with a few colleagues to international conferences about wearable electronics, in order to make contact with people to possibly collaborate with. Nine times out of ten the technicians looked at us as though we were from another planet. We tried to explain to them: "You are making things for people to wear but as items of clothing they really don't look very good. You should try collaborating with a fashion designer so then you can create something beautiful." They really didn't understand why they needed a designer. And five or eight years later we were being asked to speak at these sorts of events. The situation has completely switched around.'

How did the collaboration with David Hepworth come about?

'David's way of working – he's a scientist – is miles away from what I'm used to in the fashion branch. People in fashion are used to collaborating. But a scientist or chemist has never learned to work creatively like designers do. A designer first of all wants to know how something feels and looks like, while a scientist wants to know how the material behaves and what happens when certain tests are carried out. The two parties should see to it that they come together in a particular way.'

What role do fashion schools play in stimulating collaboration between different disciplines?

'I think that in recent years, if you look at the courses or traditional parts of the curriculum, then schools more and more often have a component in which collaboration between disciplines is stimulated. But I think that there are also a lot of designers who are starting to see that this is an important development. It's a sort of snowball effect – the more you start seeing this, the more people are inspired by it. There still has to be a lot more collaborating, but at least a start has been made.'

There is a lot of overproduction and a lot of clothes are dumped. What changes do you see in the current methods of recycling?

'Just like other industries, the fashion industry should be obliged to take responsibility for the environment. In the car industry, for example, leftover parts can be sent back to the producer. If fashion companies had to take responsibility for the quantities that they produce, then I think we would see a new way of thinking about fashion and fashion production. We should all become more aware. We cannot keep consuming the way we do now, it's not sustainable.'

One of the things you talk about in your book is 3D Printing. With this technique there's no reason for overproduction since you make only what you need. What do you think about this idea?

'It's an exciting development that's bound to happen. It will cause an enormous shift in production and consumption. I don't understand why more companies are not worrying about the future, since this technique will influence large sectors of the industry and make them disappear. As power comes to lie with those who possess the technology, large companies will lose their right to exist. Everyone can design a garment at home and simply have it produced by someone with the right equipment. All the developments in my book represent new ways of looking at our wardrobes and at what we are actually wearing. We are seeing the formation of a critical mass of designers and researchers from all over the world who are looking into these new possibilities, although it is still largely taking place in the realm of research.'

What would you like to develop in the next ten years?

'If you're talking about materials then ten years is not very long. Since Lycra there's not been any other material that's had such an impact on fashion. And Lycra came on the market fifty years ago. In any case, my fantasy material will cause no damage to man or environment prior to, during or after production. Finding a 100 % durable material, one that is also beautiful and commercial, that's the "Holy Grail" at this moment.'

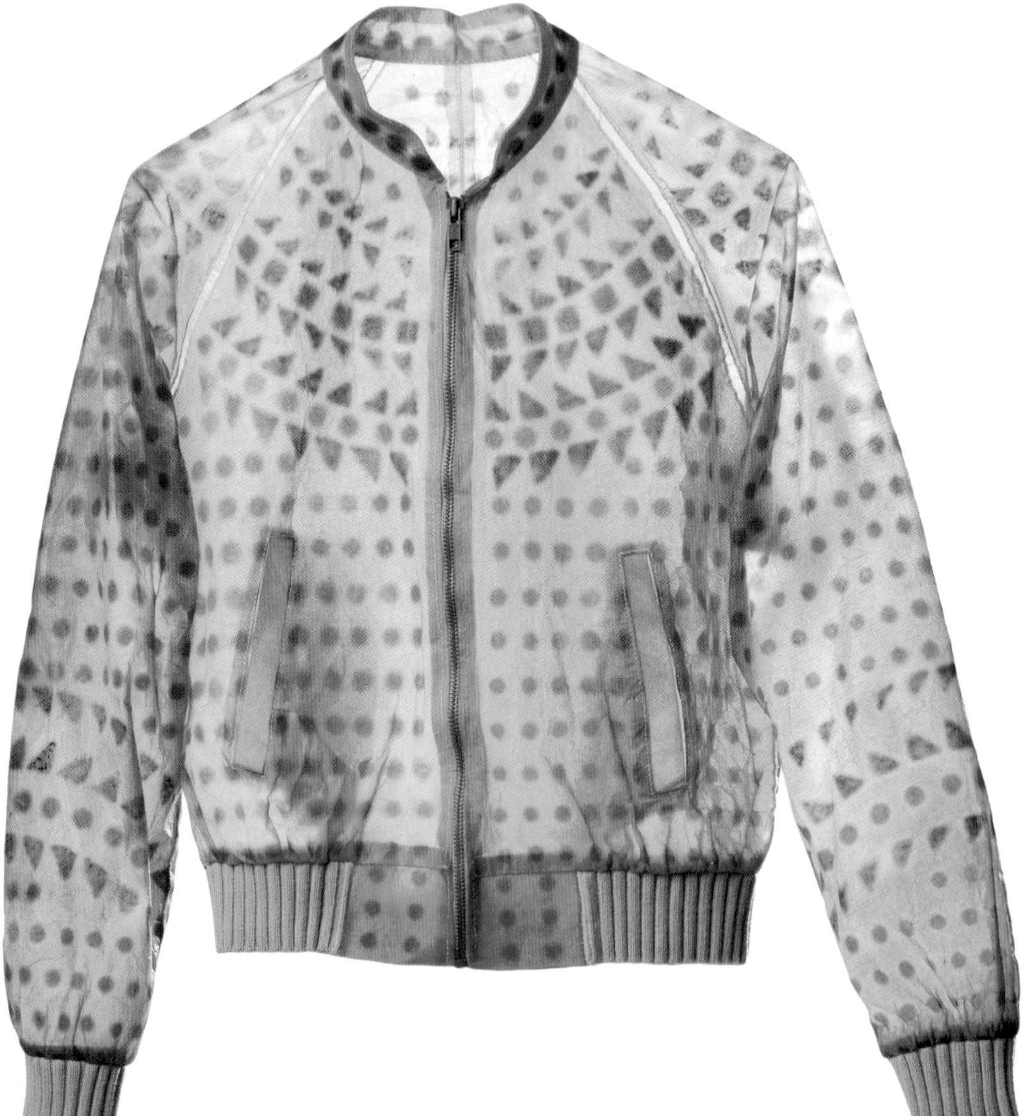

SUZANNE L
INSTALLATIC
FORT ASPERE
20

'IMAGINE IF WE COULD GROW CLOTHING...'

The BioCouture research project aims to address the urgent need for more sustainable approaches in textiles/fashion. Bio-Couture is harnessing nature to propose a radical future fashion vision. We are investigating the use of bacterial cellulose, grown in a laboratory, to produce clothing.

A harmless bacteria (*Acetobacter xylinum*) spins pure cellulose fibres when fed a glucose solution. This bacteria produces cellulose and simultaneously spins it into a sheet of material. Using bacteria to directly manufacture a fabric removes several stages from textile production. Rather than harvest cotton, clean and spin fibres and use a machine to weave or knit it into a cloth, BioCouture asks: 'What if we could use the bacteria itself to perform the entire process?' Our ultimate goal is to literally grow a dress in a vat of liquid...

The images shown here document some of the stages of Bio-Couture production, from a vat of sugary tea to three jackets sewn from bacterial cellulose harvested in the laboratory.

For more information please see www.biocouture.co.uk

This research is supported by the Arts and Humanities Research Council.

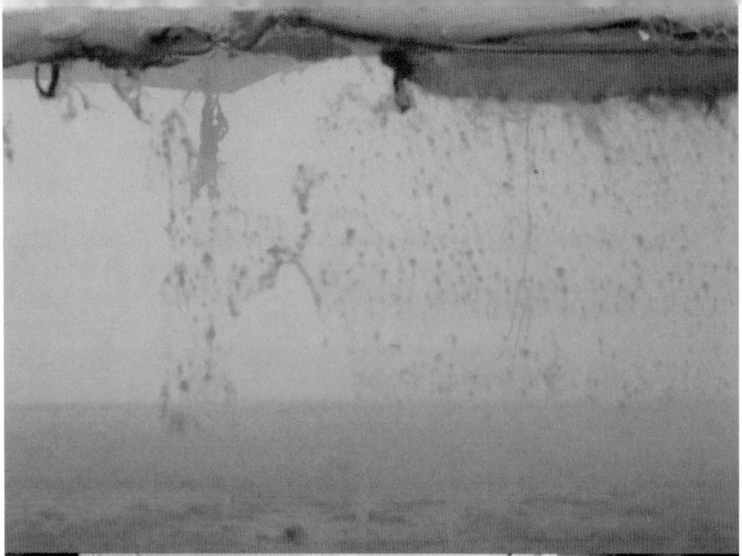
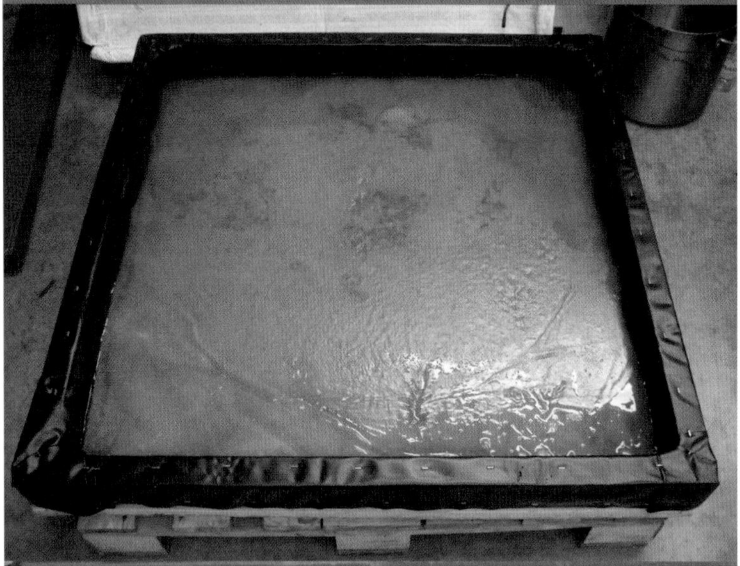
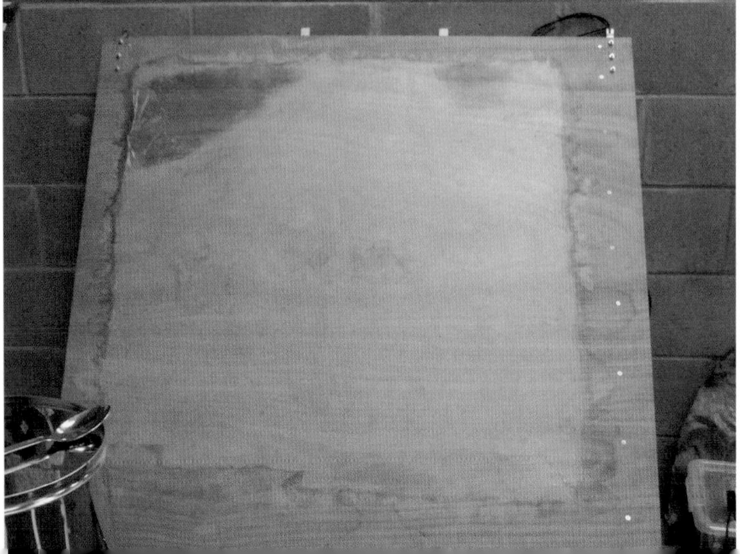

JOSÉ TEUNISSEN

peter
olsen

109
PETER
INGWERSEN

'YOU DON'T BUY ANOTHER JACKET OR DRESS BECAUSE YOU NEED IT, BUT TO MAKE YOU LOOK ATTRACTIVE.'

'I suddenly got the idea while standing under the shower in Paris. I'd just seen fantastic shows at the Prêt-à-Porter and had gone shopping afterwards. Overwhelmed by all those beautiful designs, I thought to myself, what if I were to launch my own label? How could I compete with all these beautiful labels? What if I launched a label with a story? That became the story of NOIR.'

Peter Ingwersen, formerly the Global Brand Director of Levi's, tells fluently and clearly how at the end of 2004 he thought up the NOIR label and within two years managed to make it a huge success. NOIR is a fashion label that works entirely according to the guidelines of corporate social responsibility (CSR) and at the same time has a sexy and luxurious look. This combination of sex and CSR, as Ingwersen calls it, really does work. In the meantime the label has brought out four collections and is on sale in seventeen countries. Media response has been jubilant. The label has already been shown three times at *London Fashion*, with expenses being met by the London Fashion Council, where it received an award for the most promising CSR label. Parallel to NOIR, Ingwersen is also developing Illuminati II, a label that aims to produce luxurious, organic, Fair Trade cotton in Uganda which became available on the market in 2008.

How did you manage to set up all this up so quickly?

'I've always been sensitive to the spirit of the times. In 2004 there came the first reports about climate change, global warming and consumer concerns about the environment. The emerging trade with China was hitting the headlines more often. It had not yet become the big news that it is now. But I started to think about how I could turn all this into an advantage and to commercialise it. If you pick things up early you can often make important steps quickly. The disadvantage is that you are so early that people are not yet open to it.'

But you turned out to be the right person with the right ideas at the right moment?

'You see, I come from a country where charity and development aid have always been high on the agenda. Large parts of Africa were being supported by Denmark. But that sort of development aid to Africa was and is one-way. Money was spent in the hope that something would come out of it there, without asking for anything in return. That's not a businesslike way of dealing with money, since nobody is then responsible for what happens and there's no obligation to do anything in return. It seemed to me that the time was ripe for a new approach. What if we radicalise development aid by doing business with it? It turned out to work immediately, since when you start talking about money in the Third World, then people pay attention right away. People wonder if they can make money from it themselves. And if you can then convince people that they can earn money from something that they themselves had not seen the potential of, then you're getting somewhere. That goes for private investors in Africa as well as for Third World governments. So what I did was to turn the thing around. The combination of spirit of the times and a businesslike approach - these were the two things that led to the start of the adventure.'

How did you come by the investors to enable you to set up the company so professionally?

'Well, that was very easy. Really, exceptionally easy. In December 2004, two months before setting up NOIR, I was visiting the designer Rogan who had been asked by Bono and his wife Ali Hewson to create Edun. Their plans hadn't been made public but via my network I knew that they were planning to set up the ecological label Edun. I was nervous, as I wanted to launch my own CSR brand and thought that they were beginning with a similar luxury brand. They were nervous, as they were assuming that, with my jeans background, I wanted to press on with ecological jeans. We sat together in a room full of lawyers and advisors. Nobody was able to speak openly, but it gradually became clear that they were planning a jeans line and I told them that I wanted to launch a luxury brand. Relieved, we agreed that we would support each other's initiatives as much as possible the coming years. The same evening I was having dinner with the editor-in-chief of *Harper's Bazaar*. She said, phone me if you need me. And six months later she devoted four pages to NOIR. So even before the label was on the market I was getting loads of publicity. This meant that I not only attracted the attention of other media, but financial backers were also coming up to me. It took me only six months to get the financial backing nicely arranged. And these financiers turned out to be such fantastic people... The very first one had already invested in a genetically modified grass project for Africa. This grass is green as usual, but if you sow it in places where there's a little bit of iron in the soil then it immediately turns red. In this way it unfailingly indicates where land mines are buried. A fantastic idea. He was the first one to hear about my plan and he asked me if he could come by in order to invest in NOIR. The next important investor I met in Great Britain at a Christmas dinner in 2005 – my company was then ten months old. When I told the lady sitting next to me what I did she asked if she could put money into it. She and her husband completely believed in these sorts of sustainable investments. It all happened via the media and the rumour circuit. I didn't have to do anything for it. We were really carried along by people who also became inspired.'

And the story goes on like this?
'Certainly. Two months later, early in 2006, I flew to Uganda, where a friend of mine was doing interesting things. Via his network I had talks with the President of Uganda's advisor, the Minister of Agriculture and the CEO of the cotton industry. They told me that Uganda is the seventh poorest country in Africa. The government had no money to set up the cotton industry. Because China had arrived as a competitor in the market, they were being forced into the cheapest and most environmentally-unfriendly form of cotton production in the world. I then proposed adopting a cotton plantation with an African partner in order to start producing the most expensive and best cotton. In this way we can make cotton into a brand like Mercedes or Levi's. Why can't cotton be a brand? What if this cotton is not only organic and Fair Traded but is also cooperatively owned? With all these added values it can be sold to Levi's, Zara and H&M, so they incorporate sustainable values without having to be CSR themselves. You can count on it that these companies are only too keen to use exclusive cotton as a marketing instrument because otherwise they'll soon be reprimanded in the media. Illuminati II was also completely set up within six months. By chance the Danish Minister of Agriculture gave a lecture about agriculture and CSR in Washington and was interviewed afterwards by the *Washington Post*. They asked what he thought of NOIR, but he had to admit that he didn't know it. When he got back to Denmark he immediately paid us a visit. He thought it was so important to take part in Illuminati II that he had the Danish rules changed. Normally a company has to exist for three years before it is eligible for government subsidy. The German government, having read about NOIR and Illuminati II in *Der Spiegel*, also came to me and enquired about a potential; it is now a partner. This just shows you the enormous power of communication and marketing. With a good story things get realised very simply.'

Do you think that CSR will change the fashion system?
'The difficult thing is that the fashion world is very capricious. I'm sure that there'll be a reaction to CSR sooner or later. There'll probably be teenagers who are

PETER
INGWERSEN

smoking and drinking and no longer find sustainability cool and will consciously start polluting the world. A generation is coming that's fed up with political correctness. On the other hand a new ethics is emerging that big companies really cannot ignore. And this will also bring improvements and changes to the big fashion labels from the inside. Even though they're huge ocean tankers, they'll have to change course slowly, step by step.'

What is your motive for this new missionary work?

'Listen, I can't save the world and I'm no Mother Teresa, but what I can do is increase awareness, draw people's attention to things. The big difference between Katherine Hamnett, whom I adore and admire, and myself is that she is making CSR into an extremely political issue, whereas I see it as a way of doing business. I am trying to solve political issues by doing business. This is for me the future. You can't separate politics and business, you have to bring them together. Only then do you get anywhere.'

The combination of politics and business - is this what determines success?

'It's also important to see fashion as a phenomenon that is inextricably bound up with sex. It's always been like that. CSR will never win unless we make it sexy. When I was growing up you also had these Fair Trade materials, but they were so unattractive and uncool that there was no consumer demand. NOIR wants to show that CSR clothing can also be sexy and attractive. The only reason for buying new clothes is that you want to look good. You don't buy another jacket or dress because you need it, but to make you look attractive. Why do we want that? So we can have sex. And that has to do with our DNA, the human species just wants to multiply. It's all as simple as that.'

Satisfied?

Previously I always had to defend myself to my friends. They found fashion so superficial, but now they suddenly understand me. Fashion is no longer just about what you should wear, but also has a political agenda and there's a business story in it. I have the feeling that my education wasn't for nothing; I've managed to realise my personal ambition. Isn't there the old saying *noblesse oblige*? If you can mean something for society then you should seize the chance, otherwise you're just wasting your life.'

116

KARIN SCHACKNAT

fashion with a message

117
FASHION
WITH A
MESSAGE

HARINE HAMNETT,
OW
ING/SUMMER 1985

The production of clothing, shoes and other fashion articles contributes considerably to the pollution of our planet. What's more, these production processes often take place in third world countries under abominable labour conditions based on ruthless exploitation. Many workers are exposed to all sorts of serious hazards. Awareness about this is gradually getting through to all those involved in the field of fashion. As a result, it is now expected of businesses in the textile and leather industry that they come up with schemes that are ethically and ecologically spotless, as regards both agriculture and the processing of raw materials. Consumers, for their part, can express their engagement by favouring 'e-correct' labels; buying secondhand clothes also offers a further way of consuming less. But to what extent can or should designers also make a constructive contribution to the welfare of man, animals and the planet by means of their work? Is explicit language necessary in this area?

The English fashion designer Katharine Hamnett thinks it is. Her name evokes memories of the controversial photograph from 1984 in which, dressed in informal white cotton and gym shoes, she is seen shaking hands with Margaret Thatcher at a British government reception. Her oversized T-shirt bears the slogan '58% DON'T WANT PERSHING'. The whole world thus got to know that the majority of the population was against the stationing of Pershing missiles in Europe, which meant that the British government was being undemocratic in ignoring this and acquiring the weapons after all. Hamnett's slogans looked cool and serious, a plain, black typeface on a white background. The PERSHING shirt was not the first – and certainly not the last – thing to emerge from her studio.

Born Katharine Eleanor Appleton in 1947, she studied fashion in Stockholm, followed by fashion and textile studies at Central Saint Martins College of Art and Design in London. After graduating in 1975 it was not long before she was showing her collections along with other London designers and was working freelance in Paris, Milan, New York and Hong Kong.

The Katharine Hamnett label was launched in 1979 with stonewashed and stretch denim. Her first collection was an immediate success. Two years later, Katharine Hamnett also gained an international reputation, by which time she had created a men's collection. In 1983 she was named Cotton Designer of the Year for her washed cotton collection.

1983 also saw the first appearance of her first shirts which each had a different protest slogan in giant black letters on white: CHOOSE LIFE, WORLDWIDE NUCLEAR BAN NOW, PRESERVE THE RAINFORESTS, SAVE THE WORLD, SAVE THE WHALES, EDUCATION NOT MISSILES. Part of the profits were donated to charities. The shirts were meant to utilise the lavish attention that the media were devoting to Hamnett at the time for distributing political messages. They were also intended to be copied, preferably as much as possible.

Until that moment such strategies were not customary in the fashion circuit. The label quickly achieved a leading position in the fashion world. In 1984 the British Fashion Council declared her Designer of the Year. It was not long before her clothes were available at more than seven hundred outlets in more than forty countries. Among her clients were Princess Diana, Faye Dunaway and Madonna. In the meantime her first major advertising campaign had been launched, photographed by Ellen von Unwerth.

In 1989 she started producing in Italy under licence. It was then that she also began investigating the influence of the clothing and textile industry on the environment and the working conditions of cotton farmers. And dreadful facts revealed themselves. Katharine Hamnett attempted to introduce changes in this by launching her CLEAN UP OR DIE collection, and she urged her licence holders to adopt ethically and ecologically improved methods of production. Without success. After disagreements with the British Fashion Council she presented her shows from 1990 onwards in Paris. It was not until the spring/summer 1996 show that she returned to London.

In the meantime she continued to ceaselessly campaign against forms of slavery in the textile industry and against the use of toxic chemicals in agriculture. She gave lectures, distributed written information and continued producing slogan shirts. GREEN COTTON BY THE YEAR 2000 could be read on her spring/summer 1991 collection; for autumn/winter 1993 the word YES was meant to convey positive thinking.

Katharine Hamnett's concern was not limited to fashion and textiles. She also took part in anti-AIDS campaigns (USE A CONDOM) and responded to the attacks of 11 September 2001 and the invasion of Afghanistan with LIFE IS SACRED and NO WAR, STOP AND THINK respectively. Later she took part in research projects involving solar energy, advocating its use as an alternative to nuclear energy.

In 2003 she visited cotton farmers in Mali. It turned out that they were living in miserable circumstances as a result of Western countries' trade strategies. Hamnett came to the conclusion that she needed ecologically grown cotton for the production of her collections, and that the demand for this had to be stimulated on a greater scale in order to liberate the cotton farmers from their grinding poverty and to improve the state of their health. New campaigns followed. In 2005, for a campaign for Oxfam (an international voluntary movement fighting for equitable world trade), she produced a shirt with the slogan ORGANIC COTTON CAN MAKE POVERTY HISTORY FOR 1,000,000 FARMERS.

Katharine Hamnett realised that changes for the better could only be achieved if consumers started thinking about their buying behaviour. The industry wasn't doing anything on its own accord. No attempts were even made to make production methods more humane and clean. Whereupon Hamnett promptly withdrew a large number of her licences and decided to keep a personal eye on the manufacture of her cotton, seeing as nobody could be trusted to meet all her demands.

The new KATHARINE E HAMNETT line saw the light of day in 2004, with the E standing for ethically as well as ecologically produced ('evil tongues say that it means egotrip', says the designer). She organised a new production chain where everything, from the raw material to the packaging and distribution of the end product, had to meet the highest demands.

The recently produced T-shirt bearing the words SAVE THE FUTURE was aimed against the horrors involved in cotton production in Uzbekistan. Hamnett has also launched a range of jewellery for the jewellery company Cred, for which the gold and diamonds are ecologically sourced.

Hamnett has recently been appointed as professor at the University of the Arts in London. Her efforts at realising the 'E' are continuing unabated by means of lectures and products. Her website provides a lot of concrete information about various abuses. For example: 'Conventional cotton represents ten percent of world agriculture and uses twentyfive percent of the world's pesticides. 100 million conventional cotton farmers, from Russia to South Africa, are living in conditions of abject poverty and near starvation. Conventional cotton subsidies funded by American taxpayers are causing poverty in the developing world as they lower the world price for cotton. (...) 20,000 people die every year from accidental pesticide poisoning. (...) Death by starvation is alarmingly prevalent and 200,000 cotton farmers commit suicide annually due to spiraling debts incurred from buying pesticides. A further 1,000,000 people a year suffer from long-term pesticide poisoning.'

If farmers were to grow organically - that is to say, without using chemical fertilisers or pesticides - the situation would improve considerably: 'By growing organically, farmers get a fifty percent increase in their income - due to a forty percent reduction in costs - and the twenty percent premium they receive for producing organic cotton allows them to feed, clothe, educate and provide healthcare for their children.' On the situation in Uzbekistan, the second largest exporter of cotton in the world, she writes: '(...) the environment destruction of an entire ecosystem, the corrupt government officials who control Uzbekistan's cotton sector are directly responsible for profound rural poverty, appalling labour rights abuses, and one of the world's worst examples of child exploitation.' Europe is the largest single destination for Uzbek cotton. The number of depressing facts is great.
The reader or consumer is urged to adopt a critical attitude when purchasing cotton goods: always ask where the cotton in question comes from, resist imports from 'dodgy' countries. A growing demand for ecological cotton is the most important condition for substantial changes.

Katharine Hamnett is undoubtedly one of the most committed activists in the fashion world. She has performed impressive work and avoids no obstacle in tracking down injustices, making them known and actively working towards their solution. But this does not answer the question as to how far designing clothing

could be of specific significance for improving ethical and ecological factors in the fashion industry. The job of the designer, after all, differs from that of the producer of cotton, leather, wool and so on. The designer is the one who gives shape to a certain image, and that can only be done in the language of the image, that is to say, proportions, colour, material, texture and so on. With applied design, such as fashion, functionality also plays a role, it is true, but then it is always geared to visual aspects. This visual vocabulary, however, is essentially abstract; as a medium it is hardly suitable for conveying anything other than visual contents. Political messages along this path are merely incidental and are only communicable with the aid of certain symbolic values: after the French Revolution, for example, the long men's trousers (*sansculotte*) indicated that one was opposed to the former aristocracy (dressed in knee breeches, the *culotte*); the PLO scarf originally testified to solidarity with the Palestinian Liberation Organisation against the state of Israel. However, as soon as the scarf became more of a fashion item than a political one people simply got tired of it, even though the Palestines and Israel still have a lot of unfinished business with each other. Colours also often have a certain symbolic value. Yet symbolism is arbitrary, ephemeral and exchangeable. In Western cultures, for example, white is traditionally the colour of innocence and the bride, while in Asia it is the colour of mourning.

According to the art historian Anne Hollander, the most important aspect of fashion is the image. What does something look like? That's what it's all about.[1] Changes in fashion, she says, stem purely from visual needs. None of the old aristocrats, not one contemporary pop star, photographer or fashion designer would ever have been able to introduce a new trend if it had not thereby met a visual need. Some trends can be attributed to economic considerations, practical usefulness or rational factors. But such factors can always be expressed in different ways. That they precisely manifest themselves each time in a specific form, the look of the moment, ultimately stems from the (perhaps unconscious) collective desire for a certain image. Each newly created image then adds itself to an already existing tradition of images in everyone's own mind. This growing archive of images repeatedly influences the perception of both old and new images.

Visual needs and the perception of images thus refer in the first place to already existing images, that is to say, purely visual information, irrespective of rational meanings and rational objections. This explains why fashion has such a bad reputation through the centuries; fashion is seen as stupid, immoral, unhealthy or simply ridiculous. Reason and wisdom have never been able to get a grip on it (leaving aside clothing regulations under totalitarian regimes). On the other hand it also explains why rational thinking on its own is insufficient for designing clothing. A rational concept, however inspired and brilliant it may be, is only successful if it appears in a visually desirable form. After all, what appeals to the public are the visual aspects, not the conceptual ones.

Katharine Hamnett's slogan shirts were applauded when they were introduced in the early eighties. The English punk scene had already paved the way a few years earlier with shirts bearing words like DESTROY (Vivienne Westwood) or WE ARE ALL PROSTITUTES (Malcolm McLaren for the punk band of the same name). But these were more like inventions of street culture. Printed slogans by designers reached a different public at the time and they were seen as visually fresh and exciting. The content of Hamnett's messages was apparently of secondary importance, otherwise they would have led to much clearer results being achieved. As far as the fashionable impact went, they could just as easily have borne a completely different message.

In the meantime we are a quarter of a century further, and Katharine Hamnett is continuing to launch such slogan shirts. The texts vary, but the typeface has remained the same. The intention may well be correct, but the question is whether you should call them fashion or design. For that matter, even the communication of the textual message does not always work out so well. CHOOSE LIFE can also be read as a statement against abortion. And anyone walking around nowadays with PEACE or LOVE from the new collection on his or her chest could easily be seen as a hippie lost in time. Another shirt simply bears the letter E. The unsuspecting observer is perhaps more likely to think that it is being worn by an Ellie or Eduard than by someone who feels strongly about Ecology and Ethics.

Fashion design, it seems, is not the appropriate medium for denouncing problems in fashion production. There are also hardly any examples of other fashion designers who are conveying a message of salvation by means of a particular fashion image. Perhaps the processing of secondhand clothing or fabrics into something new comes closest (although the question always remains as to how far such designs are created on the basis of ideological intentions). Martin Margiela's series of leather jackets made from old motorcycling jackets, for example, were hip and 'responsible'. Elsewhere you might see used Japanese kimonos transformed into unusual shirts, pumps and so on. In view of the marginal extent of such productions, however, they are not effective on the global, industrial scale.

Even though explicit reformist thinking has not merged into a unity with the image of fashion at the level of perception, this does not mean to say that designers should therefore sit by passively and watch how the production of cotton (or wool, leather, silk, gold, diamonds...) is ruining life on earth. Implicit consequences can indeed be drawn, for example by making particular choices regarding use of materials and cooperation with suppliers, clients, photographers and so on. It is possible to develop high-quality products using clean and just methods. In that respect, Katharine Hamnett is totally right.

[1] Anne Hollander, 'Dress', in: *Seeing Through Clothes*. New York (Penguin Books) 1988.

i'm not
the
only one
who's
crazy
and
clean

There's nothing wrong with living on the sidelines, but some women make their dreams come true and stick their necks out. Katharine Hamnett gives it all she's got.

'I see a canal!', she cries enthusiastically from the back seat the moment we drive into Amsterdam's ring of canals. 'I see a bridge! Oh, and the houses, it's exactly as I had imagined Amsterdam to be!' Katharine Hamnett (1947), British fashion designer and campaigner ('and a maniac', she adds with a laugh) has just harangued the Beyond Green symposium and is now enjoying a ride through Amsterdam, the first time in her life that she's been in the city. She is sixty, an enviable sixty – with the body of a teenage girl and the coolness of a Jane Birkin.

Katharine Hamnett was big in the eighties; even those who are not interested in fashion probably know her oversized T-shirts emblazoned with CHOOSE LIFE – made world-famous through Wham! In *Wake Me Up Before You Go-Go*. And should even that not mean anything to you, then you may have spotted one of her slogan shirts on a celebrity in recent months: Liz Hurley, for example, in a pink BRING BACK GOD shirt, KT Tunstall in a SAVE THE FUTURE shirt at the *Live Earth* concert, and then there's Sarah Jessica Parker who appears in a STAY ALIVE IN 85 shirt in the *Sex and the City* film. All this has nothing to do with an eighties revival, but with the fact that Katharine Hamnett's message is finally getting through: that the world is doomed if we keep going on like this. She has been fighting already since 1989 for an ethical and environmentally-friendly way of producing clothes and for a long time was a solitary voice crying in the wilderness. But now she's been proved right: green is hip, green is hot. And green is a must if we want to stop global warming and no longer have fashion victims on our conscience (each year, for example, twenty thousand cotton farmers die of pesticide poisoning and a million more people suffer lasting damage, according to the World Health Organization).

SLOGAN SHIRTS
But let's begin at the beginning. How did she end up in the fashion world? Enjoying a cup of hot chocolate in a pub, Katharine tells her story. 'It was at the age of thirteen that I first heard that I would later have to earn my own living. I felt enormously hurt. And I had no idea what I wanted to become. Archaeologist, marine biologist, trapeze artist? When I was fifteen we went to live in Stockholm where my father was the British military attaché and so I was also on the diplomatic list. Every evening my friends and I plundered all the cocktail parties for diplomats and although we were an enormous pain in the neck of course, we had to look posh. I am tall and could never find clothes that fitted me well. What's more, my parents were very mean with pocket money, so I made a lot of clothes myself.'

Fashion thus became her way of making a living. After a thorough training in fashion at the Central Saint Martins College in London, she launched the Tuttabankem label with a student girlfriend. 'We were making really idiotic clothes.

127
I'M NOT
THE ONLY
ONE
WHO'S
CRAZY
AND
CLEAN

Hand-painted suede spacesuits. A hand-woven leather gladiator outfit that we were sure would catch on. But starvation is a very good teacher: after working continuously for three years and earning hardly any money it began to dawn on me that you had to make something that people can wear and want to wear.'

Katharine freelanced for a few years. 'Learned a lot, from making samples to making sure that your invoices were paid. I'd rehearsed a whole act for this – people literally hid under their desk when I came in.' In order to launch her own label in 1979 she borrowed five hundred pounds from a friend who was married to a biscuit millionaire. 'It was drudgery, but the label grew and grew, until it exploded.' She was the first to come up with the 'crumpled look' ('Life is really too short to spend your time ironing. I used to get thank-you letters from people: you've saved me!'), she coined the term 'power dressing' ('How awful, this has to go in my hall of shame, I feel almost as though I'm responsible for that terrible materialistic yuppie period') as well as stonewashed jeans ('Can also go in the hall of shame. So harmful for the environment'). And, as happens with successful designers, she was copied on a massive scale. And adored. 'I always wore black shades at that time so that people wouldn't recognise me when I took them off. Fame is weird, psychotic. I thought, how can I exploit this in a way that's good? What if I make T-shirts with a political message, then they'll also be copied on a massive scale.'

And so the slogan T-shirt was born. A message printed in capitals like a newspaper headline – 'People believe everything that's printed, this is really a propaganda trick' – that can easily be read from a few metres distance, as though you're carrying your own personal banner. An instant hit at a time, 1983, when everyone was going onto the streets to protest about the slightest thing. 'I didn't think they would sell. I thought, this would be nice to wear on a demo, they're always a bit tacky. I wanted to make demos a bit elegant.' She herself wore one of her slogan T-shirts for a meeting with Margaret Thatcher: 58% DON'T WANT PERSHING, a comment on the stationing of American nuclear missiles in Europe. How did Maggie react? 'She said, Oh, we don't have any Pershings, we have cruise missiles. She really has that fishwife wit!'

WAKE-UP CALL

Katharine has success, fame, celebrities like Madonna and Princess Diana as clients. But was she happy? 'It's as though you're in a treadmill, you keep doing the same thing, you're earning tons of money, but you have the feeling that something is missing. In Buddhism they say that if you want to have a happy life you have to live in a good way. So I thought, I make clothes, not weapons, but let's just check whether we're doing it in a responsible way. What then emerged was one big nightmare. Clothing, it appeared, was harming the environment more than anything else. As much as ten percent of all agriculture was devoted to growing cotton, which used 25 percent of all pesticides. Fashion pollutes and destroys, dumps toxic chemicals into the environment, such as dioxines from lycra and PVC, bleaching agents and heavy metals from dye processes. And so on.'

Starting in 1989 it's CLEAN UP OR DIE: not only the text on yet another protest shirt, but Katharine tried to clean up her company wherever possible. 'Not easy, because I'd delegated a lot to licencees. I went to the producers of Katharine Hamnett Denim, for example, and asked them to henceforth give a percentage of the wholesale revenue to the farmers in order to help them switch to organic cotton. That went well the first seasons, until I found out that they had stopped sending the cheque because the amount was becoming bigger and bigger as we were selling more and more. In the end I went to them with a camera crew from Channel 4 News to force them to hand over the money. Well, that was immediately the end of that business relationship. Unfortunately it didn't go much better with other licencees. One major manufacturer in Italy said literally: you with your ethical and environment-friendly shit, fuck off.'

The biggest blow was the visit she made to Mali in 2003 with Oxfam, where she saw with her own eyes the consequences of the cotton industry: 'People who were starving because the money they were earning with the harvest went to stranglehold contracts with Western pesticide manufacturers. I met the wife of a cotton farmer who had lost two babies because she was undernourished and could hardly breastfeed. It broke me up.'

129
I'M NOT
THE ONLY
ONE
WHO'S
CRAZY
AND
CLEAN

ORGANIC COTTON

Her initial reaction was to chuck it all in. But she decided to take action. 'I thought, fuck the industry. Better to be poor than to have twenty thousand deaths a year on my conscience. I tore up all the contracts I could and sold my house.' She put the proceeds into a new company, Katharine E Hamnett, where the E not only stands for her second name, Eleanor, but also for 'ethical' and 'environmental'. She is producing small collections again, everything from hundred percent organic cotton, of course. 'Just feel how soft it is,' she says, holding out her sleeve. 'Everyone thinks they're going to be tortured, but organic cotton is divine. My slogan shirts sold enormously well last summer. I think that after 11 September people have become more critical, and such a T-shirt gives you a voice. I've designed one specially for the American elections - DELIVER US FROM EVIL - where US, of course, also stands for the United States.' She laughs heartedly. But is immediately serious again. 'You can have all the Kelly bags in the world and still feel miserable. My whole life made sense the moment I realised that the world has been entrusted to us. Those words from Genesis - "Let us make man in our image and let them have dominion over all the earth" - is wrongly translated. I had a professor look at it, both in Hebrew and Greek, and it's not "have dominion over", but "safeguard", "take charge of". That changes everything! Your life then makes sense.'

So has she found what was missing in her life? 'Yes. It's been tough, it's been scary, it was a real struggle. For a long time I felt myself to be a minority of one. But now there are more and more crazy, lovely, clean people who really want to change the world. I'm no longer alone and that feels fantastic.'

sustainability, our common fashion environment

The movie *Gandhi* by Richard Attenborough (1982) ought to be a classic for any student in textiles and in fashion not only because it deals with the impact of colonialism on industrialization, but also because of the iconic remark to me, somewhere halfway the movie: 'You cannot wear something with love that has been made without love.' Whether Gandhi said it or Attenborough put it in the mouth of Ben Kingsley, it should remind us of the importance of manufacturing as an activity providing dignity and providing satisfaction through the mobilization of love for a job well done. In a time of globalised production the values of consuming and production are often thousands of miles apart. The meaning of wearing is often disjoined from the meaning of making. The impact of fashion in terms of sustainability is also disjoined between choices of consumers and effects in manufacturing zones. Our consumption creates derelict lands in Pakistan, water pollution in China, oil spillages in the Persian Gulf. I would like to extend the concept of love to the love for the next generation: to the way textiles and fashion contribute to the sustainability of the earth and our legacy to the next generation.

Let us look at consumption first: each rich country's citizen spends around € 1500 on textiles, which is 30 kg of fibres each year. Little less than half of it is on apparel, almost one third on home textiles and almost a quarter is hidden in the car, a plane, in a filter or a conveyor belt; uses we amalgamate as technical textiles. Textiles represent some twelve percent of consumption in value and seven percent in volume. The sustainability of textiles is less a consequence of how much we buy, less of what we buy, of how it is made and where it is made and what it is worth. The first key criterion is the amount of fibres we buy. It is much less a consequence of how much we spend. One kilo of fibres costs around 2 Euro's, one kilo of apparel costs anything between 150 and 1000 Euro's. The composition of our budgets does matter: do we choose for fast fashion at low process or do we take up the 'less is more' concept of Ludwig Mies van der Rohe?

The stakes are high. While the average European or American buys around 30 kg of fibres, the vast majority of people in Asia and Africa do hardly reach 3 kg. But surging China has achieved a fibre consumption of 6 kg/person, Turkey or Brazil around 10 kg/person. Just to put the 30 kg in perspective: we have each an area of 600 m2 of fibre production somewhere in the world. That is our ecological footprint. Each kilo adds 20 m2 additional space. The total global fibre production and consumption stands now at around 55 million tons. That is roughly 9 kg per human being. Each year fibre consumption increases by 1 kg/person, that adds 5 million tons fibre production a year. That is equal to the entire cotton production of India and Pakistan combined or a cultivation area equal to three times Belgium. It is comparable to five large polyester mills or the fuel consumption of the Netherlands. Year by year we do not have this area at

131
SUSTAIN-
ABILITY.
OUR
COMMON
FASHION
ENVIRON-
MENT

hand. We cannot sustain the yearly growth in fibre consumption. By 2020 we have a fibre gap: a difference of twenty percent between global demand and global supply. If all people use the amount of fibre we do, we would need the entire surface of India cultivated with cotton. We do not have that surface, especially not as we eat more and better, as we want to live bigger and better and want to drive more and drive better. Using acres for cotton or using oil for fibres is a very inefficient way to use land, provide incomes to farmers or to industries. An additional element to the footprint is the water use. Each kilo of fibres needs an average of 2000 litres of water for irrigation (cotton), cleaning and cooling and dyeing and finishing. Each kilo of fibres needs the equivalent of an average 50 litres of fuel for energy for processing. Thirty kilo's of fibres is more than the average annual gasoline consumption and more than the average domestic water use in developed countries. We do not have that amount of water; with growing food needs and urbanization we desperately need all the water we have. This requires a dramatic improvement of water efficiency in cultivation of cotton and energy in industrial water use and recycling. In order to frame the debate it is important to allocate the environmental impact in the supply chain. More than seventy percent of the environmental impact of textiles is in the generation and production of fibre, ten percent is in the textile production stages, five percent in the clothing production stages and fifteen percent in the care (washing) and disposal of the product after use.

However my first argument with regard to textiles and sustainability is to look at the way we consume, as the amount and the composition of consumption are the first determinants of sustainability.

Let us start with fashion: with more than 10 kg per person in developed countries it is the most important flow. The challenge here is twofold. The traditional slow fashion cycle is build on production long in advance based on trend analysis, but with the effect that thirty percent of the products remain unwanted and unsold. The model of fast fashion has transformed clothing into a disposable product that can be worn five to ten times and is then thrown away. This is far below the standard life time of a garment that can be fifty wear and wash cycles in mid-level quality. First with respect to slow fashion: the share of sales at markdown has hardly declined over the last fifteen years and still stands at around thirty percent. Second with respect to fast fashion: its share has increased with the rise of Zara and Hennes and Mauritz, and the impact is that after stable fibre consumption in Europe between 1995 and 2005 it is on the rise again. This is a worrying sign.

With regard to home textiles the rise of fast fashion is set in motion as well, e.g. with the advent of Zara home. Especially curtains are becoming fashion items. However home textiles are still predominantly seen as a commodity and durability is an important feature. In volume terms there is a shift from carpets to

120 Crates of Water for Each Kg/ textile (6000 liter)

Production Cycle

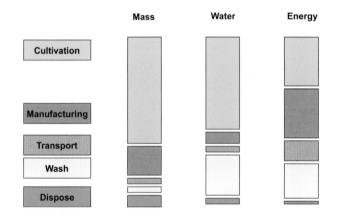

	Mass	Water	Energy
Cultivation			
Manufacturing			
Transport			
Wash			
Dispose			

133
SUSTAIN-
ABILITY.
OUR
COMMON
FASHION
ENVIRON-
MENT

Substitution 2 (energy)

hard floor coverings. While this reduces the amount of fibres used, the substitution by other materials does hardly provide a sustainability gain.

The same logic applies the other way for technical textiles. This fastest growing textiles segment is replacing plastics or metals in automotive, aerospace, constructive etc... This may be worrying, but once more the total mass of materials does not increase per se the level of energy or water. Whereas the weight/performance ratio of textiles is often better than for steel, the increased use of textiles may lead to higher fuel efficiency of cars. The use of synthetic turf may seem less environmental efficient than natural grass, but synthetic lawn does not need water, or mowing.

Part of technical textiles is professional textiles, especially work wear. The same substation exercise applies here as for technical textiles as a whole. One of the balancing acts is between disposables and re-usables, as e.g. in medical textiles. The other balancing act is on function optimalisation: that is the optimal balance between functionality required and material selection often with the aim to achieve an optimal durability.

Sustainable consumption is by far no simple thing. To summarize the previous paragraphs it is determined by the volume we buy, but also by the rotation of products. It is determined by the durability of products but also with particular reference to washing in relation to life-cycle. It is also determined by substitution effects of textiles compared to other products. Finally in many instances the choice for textiles compared to other materials has an effect on associated environmental effects with respect to water and energy consumption in the utilization of the product. However as I shall focus on apparel in this article the most important factor for fashion is the relationship between volume and value, and the durability of the products bought. What distinguishes apparel from other textile segments is the absence of substitution. For instance carpet can be replaced by parquet floors or tiled floors. One needs to assume though that money spend less on apparel is spend on another category, hence also creates an environmental impact.

SUSTAINABILITY SHIFTS

I would like to investigate the following options within regard to fashion:
- Consuminderen and consubetteren: reduce consumption in kilos by promoting durability in taste and function.
- Fibre substitution and organic substitution.
- Design and process optimisation.
- Recycling and re-use of materials.

The first shift is to buy less. As basically the sustainability is the consequence of the volume we buy, reduction of the volume leads to a reduced footprint. This is not per se the case as buying less only works over a longer period of time if it is combined with products that last longer. One can easily calculate the amount of minimal wardrobe required. Assuming seven days a week and a weekly washing cycle around ten outfits suffice, each having a lifespan of two years (ca. sixty washings and six dry cleaning turns). This works only if the freed disposable income is not spend on other categories with a higher footprint. My estimate is that consuminderen offers a sustainability gain of ten to forty percent. Hence the buying of five outfits a year may suffice, being for a men five trousers, five shirts and a combination of five jackets or pull-over and cardigans. If one includes underwear and one coat every two years, this is a package of around 7-8 kg/year. A comparable package for women may consist of more items but less weight as ladies wear tends to use less material.

The second shift is to buy better, that is to buy according to the durability of the products. This is no easy task but may be done based on optimizing product choice. The consubetter shift has a technical and a fashion component. The technical component may lead to buy products with high intrinsic technical quality in terms of tear resistance, abrasion resistance, sensitivity to stains and wash ability. The list of practical recommendations may be endless but may consist of preferring products made from long fibres, that have a low pilling, that are dyed in robust colors, that may be blended with fibres contributing to a stronger fabric etc. Although the list may be long, the problem is that the consumer hardly has the information to buy in a conscious way. Therefore the non-technical component is easier. The non-technical component may consist of resisting fashion fads, of buying according to a wardrobe-management principle (that can be combined with other items), to avoid buying products that can only be used on a few occasions, to buy made to measure etc... The effect of more conscious consumption may lead to a reduction of forty to sixty percent in buying volume.

The third impact may be in fibre shift, that is to favour products with less environmental impact instead of those with a higher impact. The realization of a fibre shift requires a high level of expertise on behalf of the consumer. In general one may say that bast fibres (especially linen) have the highest environmental efficiency followed by cellulosic fibres (viscose), then wool, then synthetic fibres and finally cotton. The fibre shift also favours rediscovered plant fibres such as nettle (Brennels) and hemp. The fibre shift also fosters the growth of biofibres such as PLA. These new fibres are attractive in terms of environmental efficiency, but their comfort, performance, look and feel as well as reliable supply and price are far behind those of cotton, synthetic fibres and even wool. Moreover all these alternate fibres advocate their position vis à vis cotton, while not all cotton is detrimental. To make things indeed more complex, cotton requiring no irrigation or additional water supply scores bet-

135
SUSTAIN-
ABILITY.
OUR
COMMON
FASHION
ENVIRON-
MENT

brennels

HOME COLLECTIE WINKEL BUITEN MENSENWERK WEBSHOP

Nieuws:

Klik hier voor de collectie

Rianne de Witte for Brennels

Winkel

ZARA

STORE LOCATOR   **FLAGSHIP STORES**   SINGULAR SPACES

LONDON   MOSCOW   ROME   SAN FRANCISCO   **TOKYO**   TORONTO

Environmental Guidelines

REDA

Bookmarks
Pages
Attachments
Comments

Home   Mission   Collection   Gallery   Quality

Dye Analysis

- 3.13 - Colour Yield for Bath exhaustion
- 3.14 - Colour yield for transmittance
- 3.15 - New dyes

Process Analysis

- 3.16 - Product Count in Baths
- 3.17 - Reading of dye baths transmittance

Chapter 4 - Environment

Water analysis

- 4.1 - pH Determination
- 4.2 - Sedimentary materials
- 4.3 - Suspension Material
- 4.4 - Chemical Oxygen Demand (COD)
- 4.5 - Determination of chrome (Cr) III-VI-Total
- 4.6 - Determination of iron (Fe)
- 4.7 - Determination of active chlorine (Cl)
- 4.8 - Determination of sulphides (S $^{2-}$)
- 4.9 - Determination of sulphates (SO$_4$ $^{2-}$)
- 4.10 - Determination of chlorides (Cl $^-$)
- 4.11 - Determination of phosphorous total (P)
- 4.12 - Determination of ammonium nitrogen (NH$_4$-N)
- 4.13 - Determination of nitrites (NO$_2$-N)
- 4.14 - Determination of anionic surfactant
- 4.15 - Determination of non-ionic surfactants

Air Analysis

- 4.16 - Measure of hypochlorite bath (NaClO)
- 4.17 - Determination of volatile organic substances (SOV) and dust
- 4.18 - Determination of number of active iodine (I$_2$) carbons

Evaluation of Processing Impact

- 4.19 - Concentration of pollutants in dye and finishing baths ter than cotton requiring fresh water supply. Turkish cotton has a far better environmental efficiency than Uzbek cotton. The strategy of fibre shift is hard to carry out and its impact is limited to twenty to thirty percent. One has to discount that fibres like PLA, nettle, linen or viscose have limitations because of their poor intrinsic technical qualities.

The fourth shift is a shift to organic, that is to replace non-organically grown fibres by organically grown fibres. This trend applies mainly to cotton, but also wool and linen may be grown in an organic system. If only applied to cotton, organic cotton uses no pesticides and nutrition with the associated benefit of not polluting the water base. However yields of organic cotton seem to be lower than with managed cultivation and cotton still needs water in most countries. The use of organic cotton is often justified as symbolic pandering to the cause of sustainability and therefore acts as a cover-up hiding a more thorough policy. The organic shift is very limited with a potential impact of twenty to twenty-five percent on cotton alone, which equals a ten to fifteen percent effect on total textile volumes.

The fifth shift is a washing shift, which is made up of two trends. First it entails to buy products that are easy to wash and do not require long washing cycles or drying. It also fosters buying garments that need less maintenance (e.g. wool) and may be dry cleaned instead of laundered. In general cotton has lower washing efficiency than synthetic fibres while linen requires more energy in drying and ironing. Secondly it entails to contract out washing to a laundry service, instead of domestic washing. Industrial washing is far more efficient than domestic washing, even if the housekeeper can optimize durability by good laundry management. The impact of a washing shift is limited to five to ten percent.

The sixth shift is through function optimisation or eco-friendly design. This shift entails the mobilization of a wide range of measures in manufacturing and product design. The number of measures to take is limitless and only examples can be given. The first example is to avoid in the design of the product processes that hasten the demise of the garment. The second example is the ammonia finish that soften the fabric but makes it also more sensitive to abrasion. The third example is the washing of jeans that accelerates decay. Moreover black and white are cheaper and more sustainable to make than fashion colours. Finally, many design effects do only aim at reaching what is called in retailing 'shelf quality', this contributes to the look of the product in-store, but the effect is gone after the first wash. The effect of this range of actions is limited to ca. ten to fifteen percent.

The seventh shift is through optimisation of manufacturing processes. This is hardly an area of influence for the consumer, but it is for the buyer and manufacturer. A general rule of thumb is that environmental efficiency improves with

137
SUSTAIN-
ABILITY.
OUR
COMMON
FASHION
ENVIRON-
MENT

scale of production as well as when integration of production in one plant is achieved. The choice for continuous processes over discontinuous processes is obvious as well as preferring proven products (that do not require trials) over new combinations of dyes and finishes. A whole range of innovations may contribute to higher environmental efficiency. This goes from better supply chain management (bale-tracking, chemical grading, vertical integration), to optimisation of material losses in production (e.g. good housekeeping and cutting efficiency). Manufacturers can be incited to use solar energy and heat exchange techniques and lower the use of air-conditioning in eco-friendly factory concepts. Investment in eco-friendly processes such as low temperature enzymatic treatments in scouring and bleaching as well as new finishing technologies such as digital techniques, plasma and CO_2 may foster higher eco-efficiency. Finally, at home the consumer may be incited to buy products that can be washed at lower temperatures. However the combined effect of these measures is limited since it mainly concerns textile and clothing industry. The combined effect is between five and ten percent.

The eight shift is recycling. Best recycling comes from secondhand use of products. Branded products (not out of fashion) can be sold in secondhand/vintage stores, and as long as they are in good physical state they may end up in the vast markets of Africa. However the times are gone that the dresses and breeches of domestic staff and children are made from the patrons clothes. Recycling is a complex matter and combines re-use of products as well as avoiding landfill waste. From a technical point of view wool is most suited for secondary use as wool can be reprocessed for spinning. Polyester and many other synthetic fibres can be melted and re-used in plastics. Many textiles can be shredded and re-used as insulation materials. However garments and fabrics made from fibre blends are very hard to re-use. Single polymer products should be made in order to facilitate re-cycling. Recycling does however require separate logistics, and the costs are substantial. Currently most waste in developed countries is burned. Many textiles have a high energy efficiency when burned. Besides technical and logistic problems there should be an incitation to recycle, in terms of price or levy incentives. The high price of wool and associated fibres is such that recycling is possible. However for most synthetic fibres and for cotton the world price should reach € 3,00/kg in order to make recycling attractive. These times will come. The combined effect of recycling is limited as recycling will always need energy and/or water and is below ten percent.

THE END OF FASHION

Fashion is often perceived as the enemy of sustainability. This is only partially the case since fashion cycles are still longer than the physical life of garments. If we consider that an average garment lasts 52 washings it may last around one to three years according to intensity of use. The average fashion cycle lasts three years between early innovators and late adopters. It is only for the late adopters that the risk exists that they are out of fashion, but that may be the risk they take since they are indeed late adopters.

Moreover only one/third of the products proposed are truly fashion items whereas basics (with minor gradual changes year by year) represent a sizeable market volume. The problem arises more with the trend of fast fashion: the renewal of the offer every six or eight weeks, with a predilection of garments with low intrinsic quality and durability. According to a report of the House of Lords (UK) this trend, which affects around fifteen to twenty percent of garments especially in children's wear and ladies' wear, is detrimental to sustainability.

Finally fashion cycles hardly apply to interior design and to technical textiles. While fashion may impact on the offer at a given time, around two/third of interior products have a product life cycle of longer than three years. Many designs used for upholstery to bed sheets are often classics or modified classics. The same applies to car upholstery and other technical products that are optimized for a much longer life-time (e.g. car upholstery lasts more than ten years).

EXTERNAL CONDITIONS
It should not be underestimated that the choice of consumers is partly influenced by a political framework. The cotton market is distorted by agricultural subsidies in the USA but also in many Asian countries. There is even no normal cotton market in most countries since government agencies are the main buyers and resellers of fibre. Moreover the environmental impact of cotton in terms of water use, contamination of fresh water, salinisation of soils is not discounted into the price. I have earlier advocated for a thorough global agreement on cotton involving a review of agricultural subsidies, environmental impact and market structure. The price formation for synthetic fibres is not entirely free since large oil companies control the supply and refinery. Moreover around fifty percent of global oil trade is controlled by states (and state owned firms).

As I have explained above many alternate fibres are poor alternatives to cotton or polyester in terms of economic viability and functionality. With regard to bast fibres major research has to be engaged in improving plant quality and in process improvement. This requires several tens of millions of investments for a supply chain with less than € 200 Mln volume. As far as PLA is concerned the polymers should be further engineered in order to optimize functionality while process investments should be made in order to scale up and reduce the price of the fibre. The investment is here around € 100 Mln, but can be covered by large industrial players like Cargill or Dupont.

The costs of inputs and waste should be better allocated in the supply

139
SUSTAIN-
ABILITY.
OUR
COMMON
FASHION
ENVIRON-
MENT

chain. This includes a realistic price for water. Currently irrigation and industrial water is supplied at much lower cost than drinking water. Most countries do not have levies for the disposal of waste water or for pollution of the water base. The same applies to energy that is often provided at below-market prices. Besides the environmental impact it has also a competitive aspect: currently the textile and clothing industry shifts to countries with no market mechanism for these inputs that may represent more than thirty percent of production costs.

The environmental aspects of textiles and clothing are not yet addressed in a comprehensive way in any forum. They are technically and politically too complex to handle for the Fair Wear Foundations and the like, and the national level is not appropriate. If the choice is to go for voluntary agreements I do fear that retailers will, as so often, duck their responsibility. I would advocate, as I have already done since 2002, the set up of international convention covering all major countries engaged in the fibre to fashion chain similar to those set up for marine resources or forest based products. A new long-term agreement on cotton (as it covers seven percent of agriculture) is no luxury for the world's future.

Finally I would urge to consider systems of levies to incite the consumer to more conscious consumption and recycling. For many products from televisions to cars and from packaging to white goods such levies have been introduced. As these levies are often volume based they would affect low cost products more than high priced items. A rebate or return could be considered if garments are submitted for recycling. I would also advocate measures to foster professional laundry over domestic laundry e.g. by a reduced VAT rate on services like repair and cleaning.

INTERNAL CONDITIONS

A shift in consumption starts with a consciousness raising of the consumer. I am not for an awareness campaign as a stand-alone action, since it is only efficient if combined with other actions. However the consumer is not able to judge the environmental impact of his/her behaviour. Even an educated consumer like most textile professors are unable to exercise any judgment. If better information would exist most consumers will realize that a more sustainable consumption (going from 30 to 20 kg) does not involve a major suffering but a set of small measures. One of them is a shift from conspicuous consumption to a more Socratic (know yourself) consumption, and to buy based on one's identity and gradual shifts in wardrobe. This is not a herculean task, but the dominant acquisition mode for 40+ consumers.

An important aspect is the lack of responsibility of retail buyers. This is partly a lack of technical education and lack of awareness, but more the consequence of a business model, hence the effect of the internal governance of retail organizations. They are more focused on increasing rotation of capital and optimizing gross margins by squeezing costs out of the chain. If sustainability is an issue for retailers, it is as much used as a reason to eliminate non-compliant suppliers than to educate suppliers about sustainable manufacturing. As I have said before, sustainability is not as yet a dominant theme in the supply chain. Hence eco-friendly design is not yet addressed nor is a global vision on actions emerging aiming at reducing the footprint of the supply chain.

141
SUSTAIN-
ABILITY.
OUR
COMMON
FASHION
ENVIRON-
MENT

COLLEEN SCOTT

toxic laundry

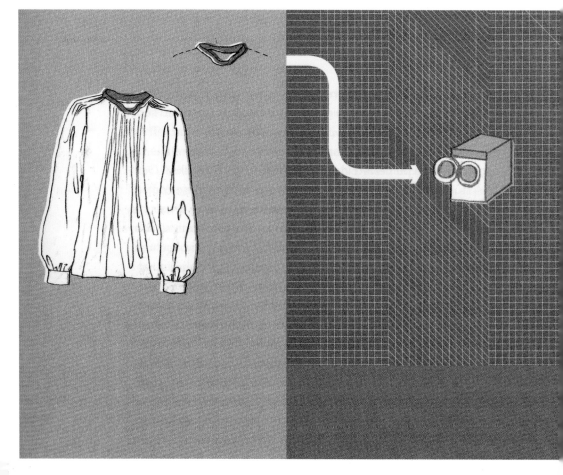

I test people for the toxicity, both physical and emotional, that makes them sick. I also look for any malfunctioning organs or systems that are creating or contributing to illness. In short, I hunt out the reasons why people are unwell. Once I find them, my job is to clear the toxicity and heal both physical and emotional damage with energetic codes that reopen blocked energetic channels. Our bodies are self-healing, and my job is to clear out anything that gets in the way of the body's wisdom and power to heal disease and dysfunction, both emotional and physical.

You are designing clothing – you are designing what we will wear each day. You may be wondering how on earth to bridge the gap between what you do and what I do, so I ask you to consider one, very simple fact: that we tend to ignore our assumptions. For instance, we simply assume that our bodies will heal themselves: it almost always comes as a big shock when they don't. You're cutting out a pattern, the scissors you're working with are the wrong shape for the weight of the material, and they're unhandy. They slip, and you cut yourself. You stick your finger in your mouth, swear a bit, and look to see if you're bleeding very much. If you are, you find a way to cover the cut so you don't get blood on the fabric you're working with. Maybe, if you're busy with hygienic issues, you'll wash the cut and apply a bit of antibiotic cream before you put on the bandage – but probably you won't do that. The cut was small, and aside from a little extra swearing when you get salt or lemon juice in it at dinner, you don't think about it again. And it heals. Naturally, without any thought at all, the cut heals by itself, and probably won't even leave a scar.

But let's say it's the middle of February, the weather is damp, cold, grey, and generally uninspiring. Everyone seems to have a cold. Last night you came home with a scratchy throat and a runny nose – it looks like you're coming down with a cold too. On the way home you do something unusual and stop at the grocery store. You pick up a chicken breast, some fresh carrots, an onion or two, a head of garlic and a bottle of red wine. You chop up the meat and vegetables and simmer it in a sort of soupy stew. The red wine is of okay if not extraordinary quality, so you gently warm that in a saucepan. You drink the warmed wine while you wait for the chicken to finish cooking. Then you eat the stew, sip the broth and go to bed early. And wake up feeling... pretty much okay, actually. Unless you were completely run down, your body would have recovered from the cold that was forming in a week or ten days. But you've gone out of your way to give yourself a little extra help – and speeded up the process.

The work I do speeds up this process too – and so does yours.

We all require clothes to wear – to protect us from the elements, if nothing else. But very often we're also thinking beyond the purely utilitarian in our clothing: we want to look nice, too. Sometimes we want to look special, perhaps we want to present a low-key and casual appearance, or we need to send signals that we're seasoned professionals, maybe there's an occasion that requires special sparkle and sexiness... But unless we're cleaning the toilets and thinking in terms of the kind of damage bleach can do, we probably have some minimum standards about what we will wear that will make ourselves look at least okay... and make ourselves feel good.

And here's the fun part of all this – it's something we don't generally think about, but just assume to be true, and it's demonstratively true if we actually do stop to think: by making ourselves feel good, we strengthen our immune systems and we improve our health. The better we look - and our clothing is huge element of that - the stronger we are, both emotionally and physically.

Is this fail-safe? Of course not. But it's a powerful assumption to make because it's so frequently right on target. It's more often true than not.

Of course looking good is a matter of taste - what one person thinks looks fantastic may make another person cringe. Some people only feel well in whatever is decreed to be the most fashionable in the moment. Other people need to dress according to some internal mental/emotional map of what they think will look well on them. Toxicity, in terms of how something *looks*, is entirely in the eye of the beholder: here assumptions have no power at all.

However... when it comes to physical toxicity - to toxic chemicals impregnating the cloth of the clothing you've made - that's going to make a person sick no matter how beautiful the finished product looks. And because this form of toxicity is invisible to the eye, it's a danger beyond the most cheerful assumptions.

A great deal of your work is being done with Bio-cotton and sustainable fabrics - and that's very exciting. But there's something downright idiotic about working with beautiful fabric created from organically and sustainably raised textiles, and then washing or dry-cleaning them in toxic cleaning products. Which, unfortunately, is what's happening most of the time.

Cleaning your clothing in toxic laundry products means that you are surrounding your skin - the largest organ of your body - in contactant and inhalant toxicity 24 hours a day. Think of it! Through your skin and through your nose and mouth you're taking in toxins on a more or less continual basis - and don't forget that we almost always wash our sheets and towels in the same laundry products we use for our clothing, so there's no break there either.

The sorts of negativity you'll experience from toxic laundry products will depend on how susceptible you are, and to how toxic is your life as a whole. The symptoms of toxicity are wide ranging, although tension and pain across the upper shoulders is a major sign; so are constant headaches, irritability, depression and emotional oversensitivity. All of these things also come from emotional stress, but from first-hand experience I can tell you that the difference between living with emotional stress complicated by physical toxins versus emotional stress on it's own is HUGE. Chemical poisoning, something almost everyone we know lives with on a minute to minute basis, is a physically and emotionally miserable element of modern life today.

Let's look at what's making these laundry detergents, fabric softeners and stain removers so extremely toxic. A partial list of the chemicals in commercial fabric softeners and dryer sheets includes benzyl acetate, linked to pancreatic cancer; benzyl alcohol, linked to upper respiratory problems; ethanol, on the EPA (US Environmental Protection Agency) hazardous waste list and linked to central nervous system disorders; limonene, a known carcinogen; Ð-terpineol, which can cause respiratory problems, including fatal edema and central nervous system damage; ethyl acetate, a narcotic on the EPA hazardous waste list; camphor, which causes nervous system disorders; chloroform, a carcinogenic neurotoxin and anesthetic; linalool, a narcotic that causes nervous system disorders; and, pentane, a chemical known to be harmful if inhaled.

Unmasked, the chemicals in fabric softeners have a foul smell. The odor is so strong that heavy chemical fragrances are required to drown out the stink. Fabric softeners were originally designed to take care of problems with synthetic fabrics, namely bad smells, static cling, and a nasty texture. But synthetic fabrics have evolved over time (do you remember your first experience with a polyester perma-press shirt?) and so have fabric softeners. The first have improved; the second have not.

Advertising tells us that all our clothing needs softeners and dryer sheets to feel silky and smell good, which might be less true if we weren't using toxic detergents in the first place. If you really can't stand the idea of laundry without fabric softeners, add a quarter cup of baking soda (also known as sodium bicarbonate – 'maagzout', 'natriumbicarbonaat' or 'zuiveringszout') to the wash cycle to soften the fabric, or add a quarter cup of white vinegar to the rinse cycle to soften fabric and prevent static cling.

A typical laundry detergent has an interesting list of chemicals too. Linear alkyl benzene sulfonates (LAS), frequently listed as 'anionic surfactants' on labels, are both carcinogenic and reproductive toxins. Petroleum distillates, or napthas, have been linked to cancer and damage to the lungs and mucous membranes. The phenols found in most commercial laundry soaps are seriously toxic to the central nervous system, the heart, blood vessels, lungs and kidneys. Optical brighteners convert UV light waves into visible light and make clothes appear whiter, although they don't actually affect cleanliness. These brighteners are toxic to fish, cause bacterial mutations and can cause allergic reactions when skin that's been exposed to them is later exposed to sunlight. Then there's sodium hypochlorite, a carcinogenic compound that may cause reproductive, endocrine and immune-system disorders, and those lovely artificial fragrances, many of them made from petroleum distillates that cause allergies and irritation to both the eyes and the skin.

The chemicals in these products build up in your body over time. If you continue to expose yourself to them, what may have been a little headache, a slight muscle discomfort, a passing bit of moodiness, can, over time, take over your life.

I've looked through them all and know of only one laundry product in all the shelves of Albert Heijn that's safe and non-toxic: Biotex. Everything else on sale there is full of poison. Everything. The only other non-toxic commercial laundry product I've found on sale in any shops *including the healthfood stores* is called Ossengal Wasmachine. I know there are various other safe products on sale in the United States - for instance, a company called Seventh Generation makes dependable non-toxic cleaning products - but I'm also trying to find out more about soapnuts, or soappods that come from the Sapindus Mukkrossi trees of India and Nepal. Soapnut shells contain saponin, a natural soap that forms gentle bubbles when the nuts come into contact with water. These can be ordered from England. They are Fairtrade, and they look to be extremely economical in addition to completely non-toxic and absolutely effective.

Should you choose to clean up your act - at least insofar as your laundry is concerned! - it's not quite as simple as just throwing out your old toxic wash powder and starting to work with something new. First you've got to clean out your machines. Residues from detergents, stain removers, bleach, fabric softeners and any other laundry 'helper' that's ever been put into your machine cling to your clothing. When you let your friend run a load of laundry a couple of months ago, and he used a fabric softener in the rinse cycle, residue from that is still showing up on your clothes now. It builds up and must be cleared out.

If you used any form of fabric softener, you'll first have to dig away any layers of product that have clung onto and built up on the interior of the machines. After scraping off any fabric softener residue, get a bottle of white vinegar (organic is nice, but not required) and some baking soda, or sodium bicarbonate, or - in the Netherlands - 'maagzout' or 'natriumbicarbonaat' or 'zuiveringszout'.

To clear my machines I thoroughly saturated a clean kitchen sponge with vinegar and wiped down every surface of both the washing machine and the drier. This included the soap dispensers and the lint catchers which I took out and rinsed with vinegar over the bathroom sink. It's a messy, drippy project, but the point is to meticulously drench all surfaces with neutralizing vinegar. Find a good-sized towel and put it in the washing machine. Then put a scant half-cup of baking soda in the dry soap dispenser, and run the cycle on high heat. Put the washed towel into the drier and run the cycle until it's completely dry. If you've previously used a lot of toxic laundry products, you may have to repeat this cycle of vinegar rinse and baking soda wash at least four times - five to be safe.

Then re-wash your clothes, perhaps starting with a set of sheets and your nightwear – that way you'll have an immediate indication of just how vast is the change you've made when you wake up the next morning feeling unusually… great! Please note that when you wash your sheets, you must also wash your mattress pad. Heat and dampness strengthen the toxic residues, and cause them to penetrate. You may become quite warm under the covers and there may be a sheen of perspiration on your skin as a result. Toxicity in your mattress pad will seep up through any dampness in your bottom sheet in the course of the night.

The problem with dry cleaning – and it's a big one – is a toxic solvent known as tetrachloroethylene or perchloroethylene, or PERC for short. At room temperature PERC is a colorless liquid with a sharp, sweetish odor. It's used for its solvent properties; in addition to cleaning clothes it's used to degrease metal parts in the automotive and other metalworking industries. PERC also shows up in consumer products like paint strippers and spot removers.

In the shortest version, PERC is also a central nervous system depressant. When inhaled in a closed, poorly ventilated area (like your clothes closet), PERC can cause dizziness, headache, sleepiness, confusion, nausea, difficulty in walking or speaking, unconsciousness, and/or death. PERC is classified as a probable carcinogen and may contribute to leukemia and other forms of cancer, in addition to causing respiratory failure, memory loss, and spontaneous abortion.

Fortunately a German company developed a method to dry clean fabrics – not just clothing, but also larger textiles like curtains and blankets – without toxic chemicals. The process places the items in a machine that removes the air and allows carbon dioxide emissions from industrial processes to fill the vacuum. The high pressure thus generated, in combination with biodegradable cleansers, then cleans the fabric. This process completely avoids the use of solvents, separation agents, and other toxic chemicals.

A law was passed in the Netherlands mandating that any dry cleaner renewing their machines must replace them with machines that do not use PERC solvents. These non-PERC dry cleaners are wonderfully simple to find here, but you do have to ask your drycleaner what process they use, making it clear that you do not want toxic chemicals used.

Regrettably modern life is also a life filled with toxicity we cannot avoid. Maintaining our health, and the health of our planet, requires that we do away with as much toxicity as we possibly can. You are in a position to reduce the toxic load on yourselves. You also have the power to influence people's thinking as they make day-to-day choices about their clothing, not only in what they buy, but also in how they maintain it.

How you use that power is your choice.

deezines

TINA HJORT JENSEN /
EVA HIMMELSTRUP DAHL

NO KAK

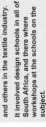

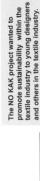

The NO KAK project wanted to promote sustainability within the textile industry to young designers and others in the textile industry.

It involved design schools in all of South Africa, and there where workshops at the schools on the subject.

Afterward there was a competition among the schools and each of the students made their own proposal. The best collections was chosen to participate in a fashion show in Cape town.

The winners went to Denmark and participated in workshops at to Danish design schools.

NO KAK is South African slang for

For further information contact Helle Krüger

NO SHIT

"Thirteen textile and clothing designers from danish design academies co-operated with a number of companies to create a collection of clothing under the name NO SHIT". EUROPEAN FLOWER WEEK CAMPAIGN 2004

"The young designers have it in their blood. They are very focused on bringing intangible values to their work with clothing and textiles. Some have gone so far as use sustainability as the theme for their final project".

PETER DAMMAND www.dammand.dk/noshit

Many players in the textile and clothing industry believe that there is a contradiction in working with sustainability and fashion. Firstly, because fashion equals excessive consumption controlled by fast-changing trends and, secondly, because many people associate environmentally friendly clothes with unbleached, undyed and shapeless items which are thus unsaleable. Ideas of fanaticism, holiness and other forms of negative attitudes could also be a great barrier. But many consumers are also open to the issue following the general trend which increasingly puts an emphasis on the origin of a product.

Today it is to a large extent the designer and the buyer who are able to change attitudes and take part in a new sustainable development of the production. Making their opinions and purchases they often have far more power and thus far more responsibility than would be attributed to today's conscious consumer. People still disagree whether environmental behaviour is a trend which has come to stay; or whether the trend is reserved for a specific part of the population the "politically correct" buyers.

Designers and buyers may therefore launch products on the market which are not necessarily perceived to be environmentally friendly and thus cater for a much larger target group. The sustainable element will thus become a natural part of the production itself and will no longer be accredited as a short-term trend. This will also put pressure on the producers so that the influence will also have an effect the other way and it may gradually stimulate more environmentally friendly production.

This is illustrated in Fig. X (The Old Model) and Fig. Y (The New Model) where Environmental Resources Management in cooperation with the designer Lynda Grose has prepared a chart describing how industry operates today and how it may change and improve.

In Fig. X it appears quite clearly that the designer's field of activity is limited to relating to current trends i.e. exclusively to movements in cultural trends: colours, shapes, styles and possibly also sales potential. The designers and the buyers do not relate at all to any information submitted before then regarding the production itself.

If you take a closer look at Fig. Y you will see that they are actually not mutually exclusive which therefore puts far more responsibility on the designer. Trends, colours and cultural changes in society should not exclude a fundamental awareness and interest in the development and production of the various products.

This process will of course take many years. Both to incorporate the fundamental awareness and sense of responsibility into the educational system but also to introduce new systems into work places which have been operating as seen in Fig. X for many, many years.

An example of this could be as mentioned in "Case studies"

about how Nike and Patagonia have introduced 100% or 50% use of organic cotton instead of conventional cotton. This has not changed their style or their target groups in any way.

It will of course require an open mind and a wish to gain knowledge of the subject before it is possible to do anything at all. This is why the designer, who has the ability to adjust ideas to current trends, company styles, economy etc., is very well-qualified to seamlessly integrate sustainable principles.

Today it is not a natural part of the working process to consider sustainability. It will therefore require much of the individual member of staff to introduce these principles to his/her workplace and/or incorporate them in his/her daily routines. But designers/buyers should not feel discouraged. Many different suggestions are presented as to which correct environmentally friendly options to make. Sometimes these issues become confusing. But instead of becoming confused or losing the plot – face up to the challenge! If you understand how to turn the process round, you will experience that the limitations can become an interesting challenge which will only make you wiser. Please note that there is no such thing as asking stupid questions – it is better to ask one too many questions than one too few! The most important point is to be persistent and take small steps at the time. It can make the process simpler if, in the beginning, only one issue is investigated: e.g. dyeing. And if for example it is desirable to use a synthetic fibre due to resistance to wear and tear, the sustainable option will of course be the synthetic fibre in stead of a natural fibre that is not durable. It is also possible to receive professional guidance and assistance. Today there are many institutions and organisations – both Danish and international ones – who are offering assistance and guidance on the different options. In the back of this book we refer to some of the best known organisations etc. that are willing to offer their assistance and guidance on organic cotton or chemical processes.

THE ROLE OF THE DESIGNER/BUYER

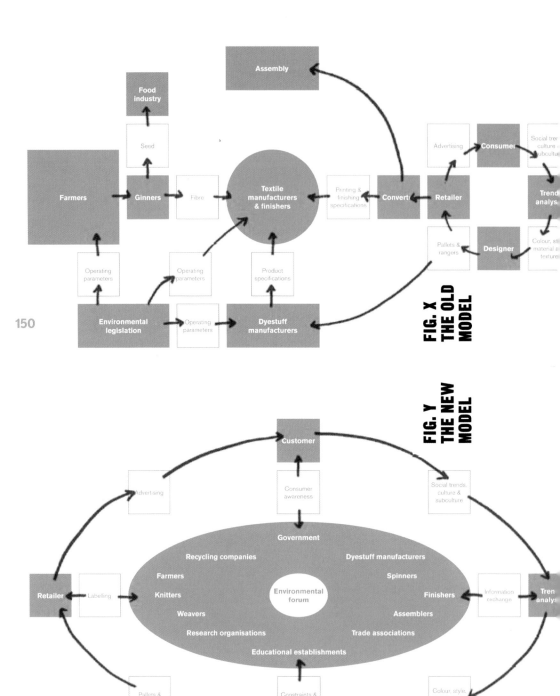

150

**FIG. X
THE OLD
MODEL**

Food industry

Seed

Farmers

Ginners

Fibre

Textile manufacturers & finishers

Assembly

Printing & finishing specifications

Converte

Retailer

Advertising

Consumer

Social tren culture subcultur

Trend analys

Colour, st material a texture

Designer

Pallets & rangers

Operating parameters

Operating parameters

Product specifications

Environmental legislation

Operating parameters

Dyestuff manufacturers

**FIG. Y
THE NEW
MODEL**

Customer

Advertising

Consumer awareness

Social trends, culture & subculture

Government

Recycling companies

Farmers

Knitters

Weavers

Research organisations

Environmental forum

Dyestuff manufacturers

Spinners

Finishers

Assemblers

Trade associations

Educational establishments

Retailer

Labelling

Information exchange

Tren analys

Pallets & rangers

Constraints & opportunities

Colour, style, material and texture

Designer

FROM CRADLE TO GRAVE

Not only do textiles affect the environment during production of the fabrics but also during the cultivation and manufacturing process of the fibres and not least during the consumption phase where laundry and disposal has a considerable effect on the environment.

It will be important to consider the entire process «from cradle to grave» when assessing a textile's impact on the environment.

The figures give a clear overview of the environmental impact of textile products made from polyester and from cotton. In the section below we will give a more detailed description of the environmental impact of a textile product.

DESCRIPTION OF THE LIFE CYCLE OF COTTON

COTTON GROWING AND HARVESTING

The environment will be affected when conventional cotton is grown and harvested due to the large amounts of fertilizers, pesticides and defoliants used.

CLEANING RAW COTTON

When the cotton has been picked, unwanted impurities (hulls etc.) will be separated from the cotton fibre. This process is also called cotton ginning. When a large amount of cotton dust and toxic fumes are emitted it can cause the lung disease byssinosis in cotton workers.

COTTON FIBRE SPINNING

The spinning of cotton fibres also cause problems with dust. For the spinning process some producers use spinning oils which do not easily break down. These oils will be washed out of the cotton during the subsequent processes and they will thus pollute the wastewater.

YARN WEAVING

During the weaving process the environment will in some cases be affected by the use of sizing agents which are used to reinforce the longitudinal yarns so that they can survive the weaving process. The size will be washed out during the subsequent processes.

YARN KNITTING

In some cases needle oils which do not break down easily are used during the knitting process and will be washed out during the subsequent process polluting the wastewater. Besides this process will produce yarn, packaging material and textile waste.

WET TREATMENT

Wet treatment of raw yarns, knitted or woven raw materials includes a number of processes: desizing, prewashing, bleaching, mercerising, dying, printing and after treatment. All the above-mentioned processes have an impact on the environment in different ways. For example any remains from potential pesticides, defoliants and other agents (e.g. sizing oils and spinning oils) will be washed out if they have been added during previous processes. Other substances which are dangerous to the environment and health are used; they include amongst others chlorine-containing products which are used for bleaching and dyes containing heavy metal. All processes used in wet treatment include a large consumption of water.

SEWING

The sewing process affects the external environment especially since large amounts of fibre, textile and packaging waste are disposed.
The most difficult issue in the sewing process is working conditions, particularly the risk of repetitive strain injuries and exposure to toxic fumes from the residual chemicals in the textiles such as for example formaldehyde.

TRANSPORT AND SALES

The fabrics and the finished clothing are often transported from one end of the world and back again. The heavy consumption of fuel affects the environment. Furthermore, the environment is affected because the cotton is treated with certain chemicals to prevent it from disintegrating.
Many resources are also used for packaging for example which affects the environment when disposed.

USE AND LAUNDRY

When consumers buy clothes, the clothes often contain residuals from the chemicals that were used during the various production processes and in some cases these residuals can cause irritation of the skin or eczema.
The laundry process also affects the environment. A textile product only needs to be washed a few times for more energy to have been used for this process than for the production of the product itself.

DISPOSAL

Large amounts of clothes are disposed of each year. The clothes may either be used as second hand or it may end up in the waste bin and then hauled to waste incineration plants or landfills.

DESCRIPTION OF THE LIFECYCLE OF POLYESTER

POLYESTER MANUFACTURING
Polyester is a man-made fibre which is manufactured from refined raw oil. Raw oil is not a renewable resource.
The fibre is made from raw oil passing through a number of processes during which chemicals are added many of which are suspected of being carcinogenic.

SPINNING
The noise level is very high when the fibres are spun and much waste from the fibres and yarns is seen. Spinning oils are also used and these do not easily break down when they are washed out later and discharged into the wastewater.

WEAVING
Like the spinning process the weaving one is very noisy.
Sizing agents are used for the weaving process to reinforce the longitudinal yarns. When the size is flushed during later processes, it will affect the surrounding water environment (lake, river and sea) because of the high contents of organic compounds, which for example can cause oxygen depletion and kill off fish.

WET TREATMENT
Wet treatment includes a large number of processes: desizing, prewashing and bleaching, dying, printing, after treatment and heat treatment. The spinning oils and sizing agents are washed out of the fabrics during the wet treatment process and various chemicals, e.g. detergents, dyes and solvents, many of which may damage the environment and human health, are added during the separate processes.

SEWING
The sewing process affects the external environment especially because of disposal of large amounts of fibre, textile and packaging waste.
The most difficult issue in the sewing process is working conditions, particularly the risk of repetitive strain injuries and exposure to toxic fumes from the residual chemicals in the textiles such as for example formaldehyde.

TRANSPORT AND SALES
The fabrics and the finished clothing are often transported from one end of the world and back again. The heavy consumption of fuel affects the environment. Many resources are also used for packaging which when disposed of affects the environment.

USE AND LAUNDRY
When consumers buy clothes, the clothes often contain residuals from the chemicals that were used during the separate production processes and in some cases may cause irritation of the skin or eczema.
The laundry process also affects the environment. A textile product only needs to be washed a few times for more energy to have been used for this process than for the production of the product itself.

DISPOSAL
Large amounts of clothes are disposed of each year. The clothes may either be recycled or they may end up in the waste bin for later to be taken to waste incineration plants or landfills.

JAN PISCAER

154

The aim of the Amsterdam Fashion Institute (AMFI) is that, after completing their studies, students will be able to make a contribution to a sustainable development in the fashion industry. The fashion industry is beginning to become aware of its role in global production chains and this is why schools should be teaching their students to think in a creative and deliberate manner about how they deal with labour and the environment when it comes to designing and developing strategies in the fashion industry. AMFI's curriculum is therefore compiled in such a way that students naturally develop a 'green mentality', one that concerns not only an attitude but also business and creative know-how.

For students of Fashion & Branding, Fashion & Design and Fashion & Management, for example, lectures are given about the supply side of fashion from the approach of 'Triple P' (*People, Planet and Profit*). The *Social Trends* and *Intercultural Awareness* lectures emphasise workers' rights based on case studies from the industry, as investigated via the Clean Clothes Campaign and by the International Labour Organisation. The curriculum is supplemented each year with a symposium (such as *Beyond Green I and II*), case studies, projects, and the screening of documentaries and films (such as *An Inconvenient Truth, Wal-Mart, The Corporation* and the BBC series *Blood, Sweat and Tears*).

It is striking that more and more students are choosing a subject for their thesis and final project that has to do with sustainable development, such as research into a possible 'Corporate Responsibility' strategy for G-Star or into possibilities for creating a niche market in the Netherlands for shops with entirely 'organic' fashion.

AMFI employs the criterium of sustainability when assessing all the assignments,

TRAINING FOR A SOCIALLY RESPONSIBLE FASHION INDUSTRY

projects and theses. For the AMFI 'Individuals' brand, for example, the labels are made from recycled paper. The intention is to use as much organic fabrics and materials as possible in the brand's future collections.

THE MUNDIAL PROJECT

The starting point of the Mundial workshops is to transform solidarity and involvement into fashion, business and community, but without any loss of creative freedom. Individual students receive input and feedback during the workshops (concept development, design/technique, marketing/financing/sales, materials, 'people, planet and profit', production, presentation, ways of working with textiles, trends, trend spotting and accessories). In 2008 second-year students from the departments of Management, Design and Branding were able to spend ten weeks working on designing a rainwear collection and organising a label with a business and communication plan. The working title was 'Dutch monsoon, Delhi drizzle – elegance on the bicycle'. The results had to be both experimental and practical, in response to the inspiring and technical sides of getting wet. All the concepts and styles also had to be sustainable and to express this. As part of the project the students worked for a whole week with the Indian designer Manish Arora on the designing, concept creation and presentation of the label in the shop-windows of the De Bijenkorf fashion house.

The results were shown in November 2008 in the Bijenkorf, Amsterdam, during the Amsterdam India Festival, in addition to a whole series of other cultural events inspired by India.

MANISH ARORA
DURING A
WORKSHOP,
EARLY MAY 2008.

DESIGNS FROM THE
MUNDIAL PROJECT
2008.

159
24H -
COLLEC-
TION
ARNHEM
'08

Collection Arnhem is a unique project that teaches third-year fashion students at ArtEZ Institute of the Arts in Arnhem to be responsible as a class for designing, producing, presenting and selling a collection. The intention is to experience while studying as a group all the things that come up when launching one's own fashion label. The realisation of the collection was supervised by fashion illustrator Peter Jeroense (*Elle, BLVD, Elsevier Thema, Fantastic Man*), fashion designer Elja Lintsen (Laael) and Rixt van der Tol (tutor in fashion design, ArtEZ). What is special about Collection Arnhem is the collaboration with fourth-year Textile Management students at Saxion University in Enschede, whose management skills support the process of Collection Arnhem.

Important themes of the collection are: the 24 hour cycle, sustainability, sexual confusion and a variety of contrasts. One of the conspicuous things about the collection is that the cut, details and volumes all occur at the front; there are no seams or effects at all at the back. All the seams and volumes move towards the front, where the voluptuous baggy effect billows in flounces. Garments undergo a metamorphosis from the flat, often geometrical, original forms to the final result to be worn.

Virtually all the designs are produced for both men and women, whereby the boundaries of male and female are explored. So there is, for example, a clasp-bra for men.

The students have also looked thoroughly into the phenomenon of sustainability, which is very topical at the moment. As much use as possible is made of sustainable fabrics, such as environmentally-friendly cotton, wool and silk. Yet the students have also experienced the obstacles of sustainable fashion, such as high prices and limited options. Partly because of this, the collection has become a proportional mixture of sustainable and non-sustainable pieces. Sustainability has also been thought about as regards form: the timeless uniform plays a role. Quality and comfort are given the necessary attention and the collection is not bound to one particular season.

The palette of colours consists of black, white and various grey tones, caramels, coral and chocolate with accents in metallic bronze and silver. Noteworthy are the hand-knitted 'goat's wool' pieces coated with a metallic bronze foil. The bronze refers to the tenth anniversary of Collection Arnhem.

Although wearability, sustainability and comfort are the most important points of departure, Collection Arnhem '08 has once again created an extremely contemporary and innovative fashion statement.

161
24H -
COLLEC-
TION
ARNHEM
'08

163
24H -
COLLEC-
TION
ARNHEM
'08

TEO STEHOUWER / TINE LUYT

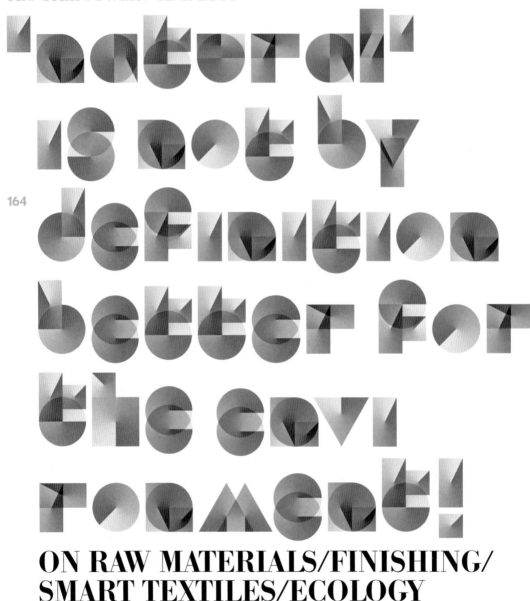

'natural' is not by definition better for the environment!

ON RAW MATERIALS/FINISHING/ SMART TEXTILES/ECOLOGY LABELS AND 'GOOD PRACTICE'

RAW MATERIALS

Fibres suitable as raw material for manufacturing clothing are generally divided into 'natural' fibres and 'non-natural' or man-made fibres. Percentage-wise, the proportion of natural fibres being used in textile products has been decreasing strongly since the 1970s. In absolute terms (kilograms), however, the use of cotton for textile applications continues to rise! Natural fibres can be distinguished into fibres of vegetable origin (cotton, linen, etc.) and fibres of animal origin (wool, mohair, silk, etc.). Non-natural fibres can be grouped into regenerated fibres (viscose, cellulose fibres made from maize or soya) and synthetic fibres (polyester, acrylic, as well as the polylactide fibre Ingeo). This classification has no bearing on the environmental effects of the fibres.

A great misunderstanding exists, namely that everything that is natural is also better for the environment. As the examples below will demonstrate, the reality is much more complex.

NATURAL FIBRES

Natural fibres originate from plants or animals. The fibres are transformed into textiles, bleached and dyed and/or made fire-resistant. A great deal of energy, land and water is used in the production of fibres (they are said to leave behind a substantial 'ecological footprint').

Natural fibres come from renewable sources, that is to say, the raw material can always be regrown. The properties of natural fibres can, however, be genetically modified through modern biotechnology. There are widely differing opinions on the desirability of this.

Vegetable fibres are in any case CO_2 neutral. In the formation of these fibres just as much CO_2 is absorbed from the atmosphere as is created when the waste material is incinerated. Therefore they do not contribute to the greenhouse effect. This does not take into account, however, the CO_2 effects of the processing that is needed to make usable clothing from them.

Two aspects that are now extremely topical, yet in the past counted for less, are the water usage during the growth and the amount of land needed for the production. An exceptional amount of water is needed for irrigating cotton – 25,000 cubic metres of water per 100 kg of fibres. This is normally not to be gained from the normal rainwater in the regions concerned. Cotton farming in Kazakhstan and Uzbekistan, for example, is the reason why the Aral Sea is drying up. If we look at the amount of land needed in 2006 for farming cotton, then it's a question of 344,000 square kilometres of fertile soil that could also be used for the production of food crops. Certainly something to think about in these times of rising food prices!

VEGETABLE FIBRES

These can be subdivided into seed fibres (cotton, kapok, coconut) and stem or bark fibres (linen, hemp, ramie, bamboo) and leaf fibres (pineapple, banana). There is a great difference between the seed and leaf fibres and the stem fibres as regards the use of pesticides during growth. The plants of the first two groups grow far apart in order to stimulate fruit formation. It is for this reason that both insecticides and herbicides (weed killers) are used. An enormous amount of pesticides and herbicides are used in cotton farming. The plants for stem fibres, on the other hand, are planted close together so that the stems become as long as possible. There is then no room for weeds and so less herbicides are needed. And the use of pesticides is also limited since the flowers and fruits are less important.

The foregoing information about the use of pesticides and herbicides does not apply to so-called organic or biological cotton. What do remain a problem are the high water use and the displacement of food crops. There are also initiatives such as the Better Cotton Initiative (BCI) which are focused precisely on conventional cotton. One of the aims of BCI is to select best practices so that less water is used in the production of cotton.

Seed fibres are obtained by pulling the fibres loose from the seed. With bark and leaf fibres separating the fibres from the plant is much more difficult. The woody components or the mesophyll has to be removed, a process that often involves considerable environmental pollution: there is a great deal of waste water and a lot of dust is created. Moreover, the process is fairly labour intensive, which of course has an influence on the price.

In the further chain of production there are only slight differences between the environmental effects of the various natural fibres. It is only in the bleaching process that we need more chemicals for the bark fibres, creating more water pollution, than with the seed fibres. As far as the other processes are concerned (dyeing, printing, making crease-resistant, etc.), the differences in environmental burdens are slight.

ANIMAL FIBRES

Animal fibres comprise three groups: wool (only from sheep), hair and cocoons (silk). Sheep are kept in an extensive culture, with the result that up to 60 hectares of agricultural land is needed for each kilogramme of wool fibres. Fortunately, this does not involve the most fertile soil. Sheep are usually shorn once a year. In order to prevent parasites from establishing themselves in the wool, the sheep are driven through sheep-dips so that pesticides are left between the fibres. After a year the wool is of course very dirty. Just imagine bivouacking out-

doors for a year without washing your hair! The wool thus has to be thoroughly washed. The wool fat (lanolin) also has to be washed out of the wool after shearing. Wool fat is used in such products as soap and cosmetics. Wool can easily become matted, which makes it very prone to shrinking. In order to prevent this, large quantities of chemicals are needed for the finishing.

The same as has been said about wool largely applies to hair (mohair, cashmere, camel hair, alpaca hair, etc.). The difference is that the rougher sorts of hair tend to felt less quickly.

Silk exists in two forms: 'real' silk from the silkworm Bombyx mori reared in captivity and wild silk. The difference between the two is greater than is generally the case between a cultivated product and a wild product: the larvae spinning the fibres in nurseries are of a totally different species than the caterpillars that spin wild silk, and the product, the silk thread, is hence very different as well. Silkworms feed on mulberry leaves and on reaching maturity they start to pupate. Two threads are secreted and with these they spin a cocoon. A single cocoon can sometimes produce a continuous thread that is 900 metres long! To prevent the adult moth from damaging the cocoon when it emerges, the cocoon is dipped into boiling water before then. Many moths have therefore lost their lives for a silk blouse. Not very animal-friendly!

'Real' silk, in the form of infinitely long fibres, is usually used for clothing.

NON-NATURAL FIBRES

From an environmental point of view, non-natural fibres can be divided into fibres obtained from renewable sources and fibres from finite (non-renewable) sources. All regenerated fibres come from renewable raw materials, but not all synthetic fibres come from fossil sources. The source of PLA fibres (the Ingeo brand name) is maize, a renewable source. The major fibre producers (currently almost all in the hands of Japanese owners) are working hard on making fibres that do not come from fossil sources. The high price of oil in recent years is a contributing factor here.

But the production of fibres from renewable raw materials does not always proceed in an environmentally-friendly way. The raw material of viscose and other regenerated fibres is derived from cellulose obtained from wood. This creates a lot of waste and, what's more, trees do not grow quickly. And it is also not always obligatory to replant trees. In turning cellulose into fibre there is a heavy burden on the environment, particularly in the production of viscose. This also applies to the modal and acetate fibres derived from viscose. The new cellulose fibre Lyocel is made according to a less environmentally-harmful way.

As raw materials, all regenerated cellulose fibres are more or less CO_2 neutral. The same goes, to a lesser extent, for PLA fibres. But that does not apply, of course, to the production process itself: from raw material to fibre to item of clothing.

The fibres that are used in the world the most – polyester accounts for forty percent of all fibres used for textiles – are produced from non-renewable raw materials. This has huge consequences for the greenhouse effect. Compared to this, the environmental effects of the production of these fibres is less important. The effects of the production process are comparable with those of natural and regenerated fibres. In the end, the ecological footprint of products made from synthetic fibres is in most cases smaller than that of products made from natural fibres.

From the point of view of recycling or reuse it is inadvisable to use mixtures of fibres. Separating the different fibres in order to recover them is difficult. Incineration then remains the best option.

FINISHING

In finishing the materials we can distinguish the following steps:
- preliminary treatment (washing, bleaching and so on)
- adding colour (dyeing, printing)
- finishing (the finishing touch: making the material less prone to shrinking, fire-resistant, crease-resistant, dirt- and water-repellent, and so on)
- coating (the application of one or more layers on one or both sides; for example: micro-porous coating [MPC] makes the material wind- and waterproof and yet allows it to breathe)
- laminating (several layers, at least one of which is fabric, are glued together; this is done with Goretex, for example).

Energy is consumed in the finishing process, of course, but above all it pollutes the air, water and (through leakage) the ground. The dyes and finishing products can also have negative consequences for the health of consumers. Some dyes and flame-resistant products are known, for example, to possibly trigger allergic reactions.

One often neglected aspect is that finishing processes can negatively influence the life of certain products. Not only through the application of chemicals but also through processes like 'roughing' where the material is mechanically weakened.

Preparatory treatment is mainly of importance in the case of natural fibres. All of these need a number of treatments in order to make them suitable for absorbing dye and finishing products. With vegetable fibres in particular, large quantities of chemicals are used. The materials that have to be removed from the fibres (dirt washed out of sheep's wool, for example) also have a harmful effect on surface water in particular. A lot of environmental benefit has already been obtained in the last fifteen years by making the processes more efficient (something that is also needed because of rising costs and taxes) and by employing biologically degradable chemicals. Work is further being done on the use of enzymes in preparatory treatments, so that the processes will consume less energy and require less water and chemicals.

Dyeing has more harmful aspects. Non-fast dyes pollute waste water, fixation processes are harmful for both air and water and the dyes affixed to the fibre can be harmful to health or end up in waste water when the consumer washes the clothing. In this latter case, the producer shifts a part of the environmental problem to the consumer! This applies not only to dyes (the same colour all over) but also to prints (one or more colours applied locally in the form of designs). The colour dyes used for both variants are the same.

The AZO decision is important for European consumers. Certain AZO dyes are carcinogenic and are not legally allowed. These dyes can be absorbed through the skin. Nickel and cadmium are also not allowed to be used in finishing processes. The AZO decision also applies to imported products. But since most clothing comes from the Far East, where legislation is less strict, environmentally-harmful clothing still finds its way onto European markets. After all, with imported clothes it is difficult to determine whether or not they contain banned dyes, as it is practically impossible to control this. The dyes used in a lot of clothes produced in China and India are of low performance; badly adhering, they also burden the Western environment as each time the clothes are washed some of the dye ends up in the rinse water.

Various aspects are of importance in the finishing processes. First of all it is a question of using as little energy and water as possible. In addition, the chemicals applied to the textile can have an influence on people's health; they can cause allergic reactions, for example. Crease-resistant products and softening agents are particularly notorious for this. Most finishing processes have a negative influence on the material's strength and durability: bleaching and roughing, for example, weaken the material so that the clothes wear out faster and have to be replaced earlier.

A fairly new group of finishes are the so-called nano finishes, a collective term for a large number of different treatments. Here the application occurs at the molecular level. One familiar example is the Lotus effect, where the nano structure of the layer applied to the textile is such that it is very difficult for dirt to attach itself. Dirt can simply be hosed or brushed off from the textile, so that washing is not needed. Little is so far known about the effects of nano products on the wearer of the clothing. Research into this would seem to be urgently needed, particularly for products in the 'wellness' niche.

Coating and laminating are generally treated as a single group. When it is a matter of applying chemicals and dyes the process has the same problems as when adding colour and finishes.

SMART TEXTILES OR INTELLIGENT TEXTILES
Here it is a question of a large number of different applications. A Google search with these terms results in an extraordinarily high number of hits. Every day sees new developments in this area.

There are clothes that can serve as computers, complete with keyboard and screen. Or clothes that can absorb heat when the body exerts itself, returning it when the body cools down (Phase Change Materials). There is textile that can release doses of cosmetics (wellness), or even medicines at a place and time determined by the user. Or a raincoat that admits moisture when it is dry and becomes moisture-resistent when it rains. Clothes that gather information about pulse, respiration and exercise. A jogging suit with built-in paraffin-wax globules for regulating warmth (the paraffin becomes liquid when the body temperature rises and solidifies again when it decreases).

New technologies are playing an increasingly important role in fashion. One very important technological development is nanotechnology (see also under 'finish'). 'Nano' means 'dwarf' in Greek and concerns all technology that works with very small sizes (a nanometre is a millionth of a millimetre). Thanks to nanotechnology it is possible to develop materials that possess special properties, such as reacting to body temperature.

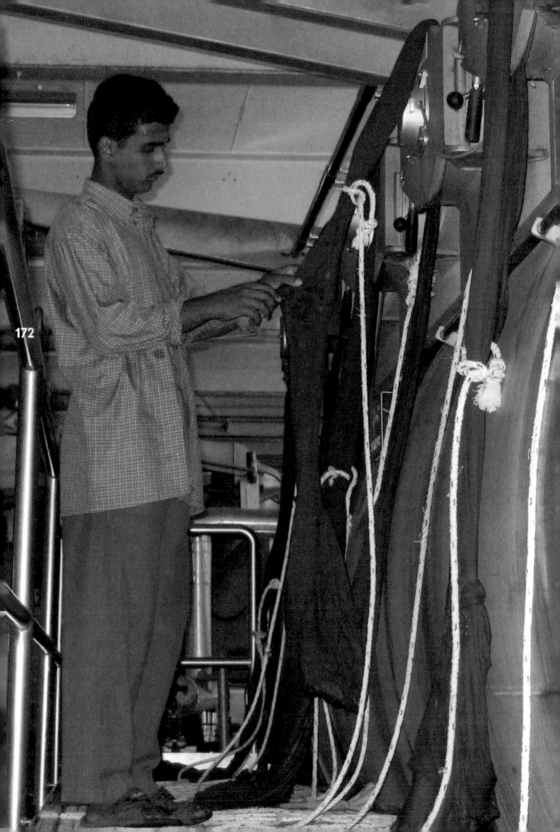

GOOD PRACTICE

'Sustainable textiles: the next step' is a project set up by Solidaridad and CREM *bv. The project involves collaboration with companies in Tirupur, South India. With more than 750 textile dye works Tirupur has been called the Manchester of India. As a result of this big concentration of factories the environmental issue has become very visible. Ground and surface water are heavily polluted, wood needed for heating the water during dyeing is delivered from far away, water has become scarce, and there is still no lasting solution for the heavily polluted sludge left from the water purification systems. With five pilot companies in the area, experts from* TNO *and Royal Haskoning are investigating the possibilities for improving the environmental performance of the dyeing processes and the water purification. Information about these 'good practices' is distributed among the other 750 textile dye works via a weblog and by means of a seminar that is being organised together with important local parties in Tirupur.*

Of course the responsibility for the production of sustainable clothing lies not only with the companies in the production chain. This is why the project is also devoting attention to communication with (Dutch) clothing labels about the problems occurring in this step in the chain. The goal of the project is moreover to come up with directions for possible solutions. For more information visit the project's weblog: www.solidaridad.nl/environmental-project.

'NATURAL'
IS NOT BY
DEFINITION
BETTER
FOR THE
ENVIRON-
MENT!

ENVIRONMENTAL LABELS

Many fashion professionals have only scant knowledge of the possibilities of clean production. Yet there already exist good standards and references for a clean process. The following are a few examples:

European Ecolabel has standards for environmentally-friendly production methods. Criteria apply to clothing and textiles from the fibre to the final product, and to every possible raw material used for producing textiles, and thus not just to natural fibres like cotton. The Ecolabel promotes the reuse of fibres and stimulates the use of cotton originating from organic farms. In addition there are requirements in the area of water pollution and the use of (toxic) aids, chemicals and pesticides. www.eco-label.com

Öko-Tex is known among many professionals. (Watch out, this label might be confusing!) Strictly speaking, the Öko-Tex standard 100 certification relates not to the environment but to guarantees in the area of health. Because of this line of approach, Öko-Tex also makes demands relating to environmentally-harmful materials such as heavy metals, harmful dyes and pesticides. Öko-Tex 1000 standard is actually a genuine environmental label, with the Öko-Tex 100 control expanded to the entire process (energy and water, as well as social aspects). www.oeko-tex.com

Global Organic Textile Standard (GOTS)

The aim of the standard is to define requirements to ensure the organic status of textiles, from harvesting of the raw materials, through environmentally and socially responsible manufacturing up to labelling in order to provide a credible assurance to the end consumer. This standard for organic textiles covers the production, processing, manufacturing, packaging, labelling, exportation, importation and distribution of all natural fibres. The final products may include, but are not limited to fibre products, yarns, fabrics and clothes. The standards focus on compulsory criteria only. First of all, the fibres should be natural and have to be grown in an organic way, based on the production standards such as those laid down in the EEC Regulation No. 2092/91 (European Union), or NOP Regulations (National Organic Program, United States of America). Second, the entire production process should be taken into account. This means that every processing step must meet certain criteria. The criteria for the production process are laid down in the Global Organic Textile Standards (GOTS). They encompass every process-step of textile production (spinning, weaving, washing, etc.) and for every step it is laid down which processing aids may (not) be used, in order to gain as much environmental profit as possible. The program also has a social paragraph. www.global-standard.org

Control Union Certifications (CUC, formerly Skal International)

Since 2002 Control Union Certifications has been involved in the certification of so-called Sustainably produced textile. Sustainably produced textile contains organic cotton which is produced in accordance with EEC-Regulation No. 2092/91 (European Union) and/or the National Organic Program (United States of America) depending on the final destination of the textiles.

The company offers two certification programmes for sustainable textile production.

1. **EKO** Sustainable Textile certification using the Global Organic Textile Standards (GOTS). The EKO certification will very shortly be replaced by the GOTS logo. The EKO norm has already been replaced by gots. The EKO label is becoming more widely used. www.ekolabel.com

Synthetic pesticides and herbicides are not permitted in the organic farming of natural fibres, nor are genetically modified organisms and artificial fertiliser. The EKO certification also makes demands of the further processing of natural fibres into textile and clothing. EKO makes demands as well in the area of workers' rights, relating to such matters as minimum wages, availability of sanitary facilities for the workers and a ban on child labour.

2. **Organic Exchange** Certification, a non-profit business organization focused on facilitating the growth of organic agriculture, with a specific focus on increasing the production and use of organically-grown fibres such as cotton. Working globally, this standard encompasses all the criteria set out by GOTS but strongly emphasises and practises its responsibility not only to offer a quality certification, but also to support and educate each participant in the supply chain from the farmer through to the retailer and consumer. www.organicexchange.org

The Supply of dyes and processing aids module of Control Union is not a real certification programme. Rather, it is an assessment of conformity to the Sustainable Textile programme for specific dyes and processing aids that are used in the production of textile and textile products. www.controlunion.com

175
'NATURAL'
IS NOT BY
DEFINITION
BETTER
FOR THE
ENVIRON-
MENT!

GEERT-JAN DAVELAAR / FLORIS DE GRAAD

FAIR FASHION: TOWARDS AN ETHICAL CLOTHING INDUSTRY

There is something structurally wrong in the clothing industry. Millions of people in low-wage countries are working under bad conditions while producing our clothing. If a clothing company wants to do its best to improve the working conditions of its suppliers, the first step is to adopt a code of conduct, whereby a company imposes rules on itself and others, which are signed by everyone. The company then expects its employees and partners to abide by these rules.

THE GENESIS OF CODES OF CONDUCT

At the end of the nineties, social organisations, consumers and trade unions started to raise questions about the conditions under which clothing is made. Companies often first denied that abuses were occurring in their supply chain and declared that they were not responsible for the working conditions in the factories that were producing for them. It was only after increased pressure that this attitude changed: companies admitted the abuses and accepted their responsibility. This responsibility usually took the form of adopting a code of conduct. This then gave rise to a forest of different codes, causing a great deal of confusion as all these codes had a different content and a different formulation. It would be a lot clearer if companies would keep to a standard code that applies to every person and to every business.

EXISTING STANDARDS

The Universal Declaration of Human Rights defines the basic rights of all people and is accepted by the United Nations. The articles in the declaration relating to work have been further elaborated and standardised by a UN agency, the International Labour Organization (ILO). Governments and businesses are supposed to abide by this standard, but unfortunately some countries have not signed it and there is no international body to control compliance. A good code of conduct contains at least the basic ILO norms.

The following are the basic ILO norms:
- **no forced labour**
- **no discrimination**
- **no child labour**
- **freedom of (trade) association and the right to collective labour negotiations**
- **a wage that covers the basic needs of a family**
- **no excessive overtime**
- **a healthy and safe place of work**
- **a legal employment contract.**

FROM PAPER TO PRACTICE

In some cases codes of conduct are too vague. So vague that they seem mainly intended to reassure the consumer. But the more well-considered codes also mean little if there is no control over compliance. Closer inspection shows that the majority of factories are not meeting the codes of conduct laid down by the customers. There is thus a yawning gulf between paper and practice, between the intentions of the customers and the situation on the factory floor.

CONTROL AND VERIFICATION: DOING WHAT YOU PROMISE

After a company has declared via a code of conduct that it will not tolerate violations of workers' rights, it then has to suit the action to the word. In practice this is controlled by means of a social audit, which means that a control takes place in the factory itself in order to determine whether the standards laid down in the code of conduct are being adhered to.

An audit comprises three elements:

- **Access to documentation:** pay slips, timekeeping, contracts and other relevant documentation are looked at.
- **Inspection of the factory:** health and safety aspects are looked at on the shop floor and the workers are observed.
- **Holding interviews:** these are usually held with both managers and supervisors as well as with workers. With the latter group it is important that the interviews take place outside the workplace. This makes it a lot more likely that the workers are able to speak freely.

These three parts can be carried out in many different ways. The one audit bureau will take a few hours, the other a number of days. The choice is between fast or meticulous.

WORKING TOGETHER IN MSIS

Since more and more companies are finding out that the practice of corporate social responsibility (CSR) and the solving of problems are complicated matters, initiatives have been launched whereby various parties work together on solutions. In these Multi Stakeholder Initiatives (MSIs), companies, trade unions and social organisations – the different stakeholders – work together on a more structured way of improving working conditions.

One example of such a MSI is the Fair Wear Foundation (FWF). FWF participants work on improving working conditions in factories from which they purchase clothing. The first step is signing the FWF code of conduct. Participants are expected to comply with the code of conduct. Together with local organisations, FWF verifies whether companies are actually doing this. Participation in a MSI makes the code of conduct credible.

There are various such organisations worldwide. They differ in the degree to which their policy is effective and the amount of support they gain.

PURCHASING METHOD
The purchasing practice is the core of a company's policy as well as of corporate social responsibility. We can only understand where things go wrong if we also look at the purchasing practice of the clothing label.

REDUCTION OF PURCHASE PRICES
Manufacturers, of course, have always had to distinguish themselves in terms of quality, price and delivery time. Yet particularly as regards price and delivery time there have been rapid developments in the last decade, which have left their mark on conditions on the shop floor. Competition in the clothing market is cutthroat. While many products and services have become more expensive in recent years, the price that clothing labels pay to their suppliers has stayed the same or even fallen.

SHORTENING OF DELIVERY TIMES
At the sane time delivery times have become considerably shorter. Some factories report that the delivery time has gone down in the last few years from ninety to sixty or sometimes even forty-five days. 'Fast fashion' has made its entry onto the market. Zara's production cycle, for example, takes an average of four to five weeks, ten days of which are devoted to the actual sewing together of the garments.

CONSEQUENCES FOR WAGES
It is not difficult to imagine what consequences these two trends have for clothing workers. Those people not prepared to pay a reasonable price for a garment should not expect that clothing workers take home acceptable wages. Whoever places an order that should have been delivered yesterday is promoting overtime.

THE FACTORY OWNER'S DILEMMA
Even the factory owner who is indeed prepared to invest in his personnel and to pay acceptable wages sees himself faced with the problem that the price paid for his product hardly permits this. Whereas the better customers do demand decent working conditions.

PURCHASE GUARANTEES
But the clothing manufacturer who invests in a safer and healthier workplace and wants to offer workers a fixed contract will certainly want to be sure that he can earn back his investment in the future. It is important for him to know that his customers will also continue to place orders in the future. Many clothing labels do not

want to give that guarantee and are always looking for the cheapest manufacturer who is then saddled with a code of conduct that may not be possible to realise.

YOU CAN'T DO THAT!

A company exists by virtue of the customer. A clothing label is dependent on the people who enter the shop, just as a factory in China is dependent on its customers, the label companies. The consumer thus has the power, since he or she ultimately determines what is presented in the shop and how it is produced.

Today's customer is critical and asks more and more questions: who made these trousers? How much work went into making these shoes? Who makes a profit from this T-shirt? And where does that money go to exactly?

Until now the fashion branch has had no clear answers to these questions. But for customers, and for more and more companies, these questions are becoming increasingly important. Customers are aware of the abuses in the clothing industry and are demanding clothing that is produced more fairly. A company can't get round that and will have to react adequately.

That is the choice that professionals in the fashion branch have, their responsibility. The decisions they take have an influence on millions of people in the production chain. If they now seize the chance to really make changes to the way in which clothing is made, then millions of people can be helped in the short term, while ensuring a fair industry in the long term.

A NUMBER OF EXAMPLES OF MSIS AND CERTIFICATION INITIATIVES:

Jo-In
Joint initiative by various MSIs and other organisations to achieve a shared code of conduct and to exchange best practices. www.jo-in.org

Social Accountability International (SAI)
Developer of the SA8000 standard. SA8000 is a system that enables factories to obtain certification with regard to good working conditions. A clothing label can choose to buy from SA8000 certified suppliers or to stimulate its own factories to obtain certification. The SA8000 criteria are based on the ILO norms and UN treaties and the ISO9000 quality system. More than seven hundred producers worldwide have been certified, including many clothing manufacturers. A list is available online. See further www.sa-intl.org

made by is a partnership between fashion labels and producers. The aim of the network is to improve social and environmental conditions relating to production. Fashion labels affiliated with Made By may purchase from flagship production chains from Peru, Uganda/Tunisia and India. These model chains distinguish themselves through SA8000 certification and the use of organic cotton. Read more at www.made-by.nl

Ethical Trading Initiative (ETI) England. This is an alliance of companies, non-governmental organisations (NGOs) and trade union organisations to promote and improve the implementation of corporate codes of practice which cover their supply-chain working conditions. The ultimate goal is to ensure that the working conditions of workers producing for the UK market meet or exceed international labour standards. www.ethicaltrade.org

Fair Labor Association (FLA)
An American collaboration of companies and social organisations that attempts to improve working conditions in affiliated companies. www.fairlabor.org

Worker Rights Consortium (WRC)
An independent American organisation that investigates working conditions in factories and devotes itself to improving them. www.workersrights.org

BSCI, the European Business Social Compliance Initiative, manages a simplified version of the SA8000 standard. Most of the members of the Association of Textile Chain Stores (VGT), including chains such as HEMA and V&D, are affiliated with it. Read more on the website www.bsci-eu.org

The Clean Clothes Campaign
The Clean Clothes Campaign wants to improve working conditions in the clothing industry. It is aimed at consumers, making them aware through information and actions; at the retail trade, which is held responsible for the way in which the clothing it orders is manufactured; and on the political level in terms of major purchasing and legislation. The website provides information about major companies, urgent appeals and reports on all sorts of matters relating to workers in the clothing industry. www.cleanclothes.org

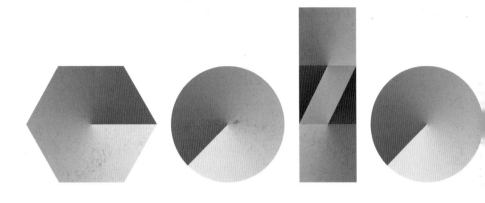

Editors: Jan Brand, Tine Luyt, Minke Vos
Authors: Karim Benammar, Matthijs Boelee, Michael Braungart, Jacqueline Cramer, Geert-Jan Davelaar, Floris de Graad, Eva Himmelstrup Dahl, Tina Hjort Jensen, Miranda Hoogervorst, Suzanne Lee, Ilonka Leenheer, Tine Luyt, William McDonough, Jan Piscaer, Karin Schacknat, Michiel Scheffer, Colleen Scott, David Shah, Teo Stehouwer, Jan Teunen, José Teunissen, Marieke Weerdesteijn

Correction: Lucy Klaassen
Translation: Michael Gibbs

Design: www.overburen.nl

Printing and colour separation: Flevodruk Harderwijk

Cover image: Material Sense

The DVD was produced by IMAGOMAGIE (Arjen Boorsma & Evert Maliangkay), Rotterdam 2008.

-The second part of the article 'Autism in fashion' by José Teunissen originally appeared in Guus Beumer and José Teunissen (ed.), *de nieuwe Kleren. Over modevormgeving en ecologie,* Amsterdam (De Balie) 1993, pp. 41-61.
-The article 'Abundance and scarcity. Concepts and rhetoric in ecology, economics, and eco-ethics' by Karim Benammar originally appeared in *Acta Institutionis Philosophiae et Aestheticae,* 17 (1999).
-The article 'Transforming the textile industry. Victor Innovatex, Eco-Intelligent Polyester and the next Industrial Revolution' by William McDonough and Michael Braungart originally appeared in *green@work*, May-June 2002.
-The article 'Technology and fashion' by Miranda Hoogervorst originally

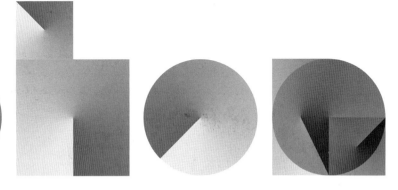

appeared, in an earlier version and without the interview with Angel Chang, in *LINK*, 4 (2007).
-The article 'I'm not the only one who's crazy and clean' by Ilonka Leenheer originally appeared in *Elle*, February 2008.
-The pages 'Guidelines' by Tina Hjort Jensen and Eva Himmelstrup Dahl are derived from the powerpoint presentation *Guidelines* at the symposium *Beyond Green*, Amsterdam, November 14 2007.
-The article '"Natural" is not by definition better for the environment! On raw materials/finishing/Smart Textiles/ecology labels and "good practice"' is based on information from the trade journal *Modebewust?* and on information from Teo Stehouwer, Senior Lecturer in Textile Technology, Saxion Hogescholen.
-The text 'Good Practice' in the article '"Natural" is not by definition better for the environment! On raw materials/finishing/Smart Textiles/ecology labels and "good practice"' originally appeared in the CREM newsletter, autumn/winter 2007.
-The article 'Fair Fashion. Towards an ethical clothing industry' is based on the text of a project by the Clean Clothes Campaign, www.fairfashion.org.

Special thanks to: Evert Maliangkay who worked in an energetic and creative way on the realisation of this book.

Symposium *Beyond Green, On Progress in Fashion and Sustainability* / World Fashion Centre Amsterdam / November 14 2007:
AMFI Amsterdam Fashion Institute (Jan Piscaer, Merel van de Beek, Yma van den Born, Liesbeth in 't Hout)
ArtEZ Institute of the Arts (Catelijne de Muijnck (studium generale dAcapo Arnhem), José Teunissen (ArtEZ Modelectoraat))
Modebewust (Tine Luyt)
World Fashion Centre (Marit Dekker, Edwin Denekamp)
Rachel de Boer (Floating Media), Mark Hugers (PhantaVision)
Stands: Lush, M'Braze, Goodies, Made-By, Brennels, Goede Waar & Co

Photo credits
Samant Chauhan: p. 167 (right)
CREM: p. 172
Peter Ingwersen: pp. 108-109, p. 113, p. 114
Metz & Rainer: p. 12 (below)
Suzanne Lee: p. 104, p. 106, p. 107 (above and middle)
Clean Clothes Campaign: p. 167 (left), p. 169, p. 176
Peter Stigter: p. 159, p. 161, p. 162, p. 163
Joep Vogels: p. 89
Dorine de Vos: p. 52, p. 54, p. 57, p. 61
Gary Wallis: p. 98, p. 102, p. 103, p. 107 (below)
Erik Zeegers: p. 90

ArtEZ Press
Jan Brand, Minke Vos
PO Box 49
6800 AA Arnhem
The Netherlands
www.artez.nl/artezpress
ArtEZ Press is part of ArtEZ Institute of the Arts

d'jonge Hond Publishers
PO Box 1115
3840 BC Harderwijk
The Netherlands
info@dejongehond.nl
www.dejongehond.nl

This publication was made possible by financial support from Control Union.

ISBN 978-90-89100-40-5 / NUR 452

This book is also available in Dutch (ISBN 978-90-89100-94-8).